Machine Learning Algorithms

&

Markov Models Supervised And Unsupervised Learning with Python & Data Science

2 Manuscripts in 1 Book:

Introduction

By choosing this book, you have made the right decision, as you will learn many new, innovative and exciting things about the world of technology and computers. It will help you learn the basics of AI and machine learning in a simple, entertaining and informative way.

Currently one of the most talked about topics in the world of technology, machine learning is a promising concept. But along with the promises and benefits, it is also often associated with controversies and debates. People who are not aware of the nature and advantages of machine learning or have received their information from untrustworthy sources often look down on machine learning and are scared of it as well. However, all the strange and bizarre things that you have heard about machine learning are probably just myths and false apprehensions.

This book will try to do away with such apprehensions by showing how machine learning is perhaps the best thing that could happen to the world of technology right now. You will get answers to all your questions about machine learning and more. So, rather than making assumptions, you will learn and understand what machine learning is all about and make your own decisions.

So let's read on.

Chapter 1: About Machine Learning

One of the best features of today's era of technology is its flexibility and adaptableness. A new scientific innovation comes out almost every day. This ever-changing nature of scientific and technological world changes the trajectory of the world every day. Things that were considered dreams and fiction once are now rapidly turning into reality. Human beings are slowly but steadily trying to defeat nature at its own game. However, one field remains to be conquered. We still have not managed to conquer the world of machine learning or AI. However, it has become a buzzword now, and the whole of the world is talking about it. Not everyone is excited about it though. Most people are worried or scared of it. However, there is no need to be afraid of machine learning or AI, as it will help humanity to achieve things that we cannot even currently imagine.

What is Machine Learning?

If you check the search results for the most popular keywords of 2016, you will find that machine learning and AI are leading the figures by a large margin. This steady rise in the fame of machine learning is because of its rising use in our daily lives. It is nowadays being used in various devices and machines as well as gadgets. However, the general population is still are wary of it. So, to do away with such myths, let us have a look at the brief history of machine learning.

As per the 1959 definition of Arthur Samuel, machine learning can be defined as a process of inputting data to the computer systems in a way that the computer will learn the ability to process and perform the activity in the future without being explicitly programmed or being fed with similar or extra data. What this means in simple words is that it will allow computers to develop a 'mind' of their own and allow them to "think." Sounds scary but it isn't.

If computers are provided with the ability to think, they become smarter and thus easier to use. Their functionality will increase by a large margin, and they become an integral asset for humanity. Machine learning can be used in almost all the fields of epistemology. Right now, it is being used in areas such as cheminformatics, computational anatomy, gaming, adaptive websites, natural language processing, robot movement and locomotion, medical diagnosis, sequence mining, behavior analysis, linguistics, translation, fraud detection, etc. The list goes on.

History:

The history of machine learning can be traced to the birth of another related field- AI or artificial intelligence. It is safe to say that both of these fields were born at the same time and then got separated over time. Many scientists studying AI in the beginning slowly shifted towards studying machine learning academically. They started using probabilistic reasoning etc. Around the '90s the two fields, AI and machine learning, were officially separated, and now both of them are studied individually. In the following chapters, you will learn the basics of machine learning and how it can be used in day-to-day life. You will also learn about the careers that are available in this field as well as certain advanced topics for the experts.

Chapter 2: Machine Learning Basics

What is it that has made machine learning a buzzword in today's era? The simplest answer to the above question would be its unique, feature-rich nature that can change the future of humanity forever. In the words of Bill Gates:

"A breakthrough in machine learning would be worth ten Microsofts."

What the above statement roughly means is that scientists and computer experts all over are desperately looking for a breakthrough in machine learning and are looking for a way to make it more accessible, useful and trustworthy. However, such programs are still going, and we still haven't found a way to devise a machine that could think.

In machine learning, computers learn to program themselves. If programming is considered to be automation and an automatic process, then machine learning is the automation of this automatic process, thus making a double automatic process.

Machine learning can make programming more scalable and can help us to produce better results in shorter durations. To prove this, let us see the following comparison:

Differences between Traditional Programming and Machine Learning

Traditional Programming:

The data is fed to the computer, and a program is run. This program then, using the supplied data, presents output.

Machine Learning:

Pre-solved data and the resulting output are fed to the computer. These two inputs are used to create a program. This program then can do the job of traditional programming.

Thus, machine learning can be explained by using the metaphors of agriculture. Algorithms are, in a way seeds while data is nutrients. You are the farmer while the program that grows out of the data is your crop.

Elements of Machine Learning

As machine learning is a complicated and convoluted field, it's hard to understand its basics. It is also an ever-growing field. Hence it is possible to see new development in the area almost every day. For instance, it is believed that every year more than a few hundred, new algorithms are developed all over the world. This brings the number of overall machine learning algorithms to a sum that is larger than ten thousand. Even though a lot of variety is seen in the algorithms of machine learning, all of them are based on three basic concepts that are as follows.

This concept deals with the representation of knowledge. It deals with how the knowledge can be represented, what is necessary to represent the knowledge etc. Some examples of representation include sets of rules, including decision trees, support vector machines, instances, neural networks, graphical models, model ensembles, etc. Some of these will be discussed in the book later.

This is the second most important concept of algorithms. It is the way used to evaluate the hypotheses, also known as the candidate program. Some examples are accuracy, prediction and recall, squared error, likelihood, posterior probability, cost, margin, entropy k-L divergence and others.

This is the third and last concept of algorithms. It is the method in which the hypothesis or the candidate program is created. It is also known as the search process. Examples include combinatorial optimization, convex optimization and constrained optimization.

Making various combinations of the above components creates all machine-learning algorithms, and thus they are the basis of machine learning.

Types and Kinds of Machine Learning

As said earlier, machine learning is complex and vast field hence it can be divided into many sections and classes. However, on a superficial level, it can be split into four parts, and they are as follows:

1. Supervised Learning
2. Unsupervised Learning
3. Semi-supervised Learning
4. Reinforcement Learning

Supervised Learning is also known as inductive learning in the technological circles. It is considered to be the most advanced and mature of all the forms of learning. This is why it is the most studied as well as most used learning as well. It is easy to used Learning type as it is much easier to learn under supervision than without supervision. In Inductive Learning, we are presented with an example of a function in the form of data (x), and the output of the function is (f(x)). The mission of inductive learning here is to understand and learn the function for the new data (x).

In this learning, the program is 'trained' with the help of some already defined set of 'examples.' This training helps the program to learn the ability to formulate a new and accurate result using the newly fed data with ease and without any interference.

Supervised learning is the most used and most favorite of all forms of learning, this chapter as well as this book will try to focus on it. Other types will be discussed briefly.

In most of the supervised learning applications, the final mission is to create a proper and well-set predictor function h(x). It is also known as the hypothesis. The 'learning' contains many mathematical algorithms that are necessary to optimize the function. When it is optimized, it can correctly predict the value of h(x) if data X is fed to the computer related to a particular domain. For instance, if the data being fed is the square footage of agricultural land, the program should be able to return the estimated price for the piece of land.

However, it is seen that x always represents more than one data point. For instance, if we are to continue the above example, then the program may take the number of wells (x_2), number of trees (x_3), number of greenhouses (x_4), number of electric poles (x_5), number compost holes (x6) and many other variables along with the first one that is the square footage of the land (x1). Then the determination of the correct input is the input that will come out with the correct result. This is one of the major parts of machine learning design. However, as the topic might get too complex and complicated, this example will only assume a single input value.

Example

Let us assume that the program or predictor is using this form:

$$H(x) = \theta 0 + \theta 1x$$

Here $\theta 0$ and $\theta 1$ are constants. The mission here is to find the perfect values for the above two constants to create and make our predictor work properly.

To optimize the predictor h (x), training examples are used. In each of these examples a value of x train is added and corresponding to this value an output value- y is already known. For instance, the difference between the known i.e. correct value y, and the predicted value h (x train) is found. When enough training examples are fed, the differences can be studied and checked to determine and measure our faults of h (x). Using our findings, we can change and manipulate the h (x) by manipulating the values of θ_0 and θ_1 to make it more accurate. This process then is repeated until the best values of θ_0 and θ_1 are found. This is how the predictor is trained. This trained predictor can now read real life data and predict perfectly to almost perfect results.

Unsupervised learning:

The data that is fed to the system i.e. the training data does not include any desired output. Thus, the data that is to be fed is without output. It is difficult to understand and proclaim that whether this is good and recommended method of learning or not. Examples include clustering etc.

Semi-supervised learning:

This is a mixture of both the above kinds of learning where training data contains some but not all desired outputs.

Reinforcement learning:

Considered to be the most ambitious of all the types of learning. Here rewards are given from a sequence of actions. AI often prefers this.

Machine Learning in Practice

Although an important part of the overall machine learning process, machine algorithms are a tiny part of the complete process. In reality, the process is much more complicated. An example is as follows:

Start Loop

Here the domain is to be understood. The current data on hand, available knowledge and goals are analyzed. This often includes communicating with the domain experts. The goals are often unclear, and you have to attempt and try many things before implementing anything.

Data integration, selection, cleaning and pre-processing

This is the most time-consuming part in the overall process. It takes almost half or more than half of the overall required processing time. Procuring high-quality data is critical. However, the quality and quantity of data are often reversely proportional as the more the data, the more it will be dirty. Sorting out good and usable data from the rest is why this process takes a very long time.

Learning models

This part, though being the most mature part of the process, is also the most fun part of it. General tools are used for this.

Interpreting results

In many cases, it is not necessary to understand how the model works, the only focus being the results. Often human experts can challenge you on this.

Though many projects succeed in the lab and are remarkable, yet the chances of them being used in real life are quite rare. Most of the projects are discarded and not used in real life at all.

End Loop

There is an end cycle at the end, and it is not a one-shot process. It is necessary to run the loop until a desired and usable result is achieved. The data can also change midway, affecting the overall process, as you need a new loop to replace the earlier one.

Sample applications of machine learning

This is a small list of fields in which machine learning can be applied to achieve great results:

- Web search: It can rank web pages and search entries according to your previous clicks and likes and will prominently show new, similar results.

- Computational biology: Can rationally create drugs in the system or computer using old and past experiments.
- Finance: Can evaluate how much risk is present on a credit card. Can also be used to send tailored offers according to the likings of a customer. Can also help you in choosing where to invest money.
- E-commerce: Identifying a transaction's nature, whether it is a true and correct transaction or whether it is a fraudulent one. It can also help you in predicting the number of customers.
- Space exploration: Can help with radio astronomy and space probes.
- Robotics: Can help to create self-driving cars and autonomous robots. Can contribute to building robots that can handle uncertain situations and new environments.
- Information extraction: Can extract information from databases on the web.

- Social networks: Can help you get data on preferences and relationships.
- Debugging: Can be used for debugging.

Chapter 3: Machine Learning: Algorithms

While discussing the basics of machine learning in the last chapter, we talked briefly about machine learning in algorithms. Let us take a deeper look at the algorithms, their types, the most popular ones and everything else about them in this chapter.

As said in the last chapter, the sheer number of algorithms that are available can overwhelm any beginner to machine learning. Therefore, it is necessary to categorize them in two large sections for our convenience.

There are two ways of classifying algorithms; the first one is categorizing them by learning style while the second is the grouping of algorithms by the similarity of function or form. Both of these techniques or methods of categorizing are useful, however, let us algorithms by similarity category and check out its nuances.

Ensemble Learning Method

There are a variety of ways in which an algorithm can base a problem that relies on the interactions that take place with the experience or environment or any other form of input data.

It is highly popular in artificial intelligence as well as machine learning textbooks to consider the learning styles of an algorithm first followed by everything else later.

An algorithm can have only a few relevant learning models or learning styles. These will be explained in the sections below.

The categorization, or to use the scientific term, taxonomy/organization of machine learning algorithms is highly desirable as it makes you think of the roles of input data as well as the model preparation process. You can then choose one that is the best for your problem to get the best result.

Although covered briefly in the first chapter, these are the three different but basic learning styles:

Supervised Learning
In this, the input data is known as training data. It features a known result or a label, for instance, spam/not-spam or stock price, etc. A proper prediction model is constructed using the training process. It is needed to make predictions, and these predictions get corrected if they are wrong. The training process continues to repeat itself until perfection, or the desired level of accuracy is achieved.

Examples: Logistic Regression and the Back Propagation Neural Network.

Unsupervised Learning
The data under this category does not have a known output or result neither does it have a label.

The prediction model is constructed by guessing the number of structures present in the input data, often to take out general rules.

Example problems include dimensionality reduction, clustering, and association rule learning.

Example algorithms include various algorithms such as the Apriori algorithm and k-Means.

Semi-Supervised Learning

In this, the input data has no solid form and is a jumbled a mixture of labeled as well as unlabeled examples.

The model needs to learn the structures that are necessary to not only organize the data but make predictions as well.

Example problems include classification and regression.

Example algorithms are extensions.

Algorithms Grouped By Similarity

As said earlier, algorithms can be classified on various bases. They are often classified by the similarities that are seen in their functioning. For instance, neural network inspired methods and tree-based methods.

It is considered to be one of the best ways of grouping algorithms and is one of the most used methods. However, it is not perfect as many algorithms exist that cannot be classified in watertight compartments. For instance, the Learning Vector Quantization is a method that is an instance-based method and a neural network inspired method. Thus, it is not possible to classify the algorithms on a deeper level with just two criteria. Hence, people often use a nested approach while classifying machine learning algorithms.

There are many algorithms and groups of algorithms. Some of the major and frequently used are listed below.

These deal with the modeling of the relationship among the variables. This relationship is iteratively refined with the help of a measure of error in the predictions or probability that is achieved by the model. They often work on the base of statistics and are now used in statistical machine learning. People find this slightly confusing as regression can be used to refer to the class of the problem as well as the class of the algorithm itself, however, basically, regression is said to be a process.

Some of the highly popular regression algorithms include:

- Ordinary Least Squares Regression (OLSR)
- Linear Regression
- Logistic Regression
- Stepwise Regression
- Multivariate Adaptive Regression Splines (MARS)

- Locally Estimated Scatterplot Smoothing (LOESS)

Instance-based Algorithms

Instance-based learning is a model that is a decision problem with examples of training data. These are considered to be important or necessary for the model. These methods often build up a database of example data. This is then compared with the new data to the database with the help of similarity measure. This is done to locate the best match and throw out a prediction. This is the reason why instance-based methods are often known as winner-take-all methods as well as memory-based learning. The primary focus in this method is the representation of the stored instances as well as the similarity measures used between them.

Following are the highly instance-based algorithms:

- K-Nearest Neighbor (kNN)

- Learning Vector Quantization (LVQ)
- Self-Organizing Map (SOM)
- Locally Weighted Learning (LWL)

Regularization Algorithms

These serve as an extension or a secondary method to another method such as regression method. They are used to punish the models by their complicatedness and favor the simpler models that are good at generalizing.

Highly used regularization algorithms are:

- Ridge Regression
- Least Absolute Shrinkage and Selection Operator (LASSO)
- Elastic Net
- Least-Angle Regression (LARS)

Decision Tree Algorithms

Decision tree methods manufacture a model of decisions that have been made based on the real values of attributes in the available data. A fork is formed in the decision tree until a prediction is made for the provided record.

They are often trained for the classification of data as well as regression problems. They are quite fast as well as accurate, making them highly popular and a favorite in the world of machine learning.

Standard decision tree algorithms are as follows:

- Classification and Regression Tree (CART)
- Iterative Dichotomiser 3 (ID3)
- C4.5 and C5.0 (different versions of a robust approach)
- Chi-squared Automatic Interaction Detection (CHAID)
- Decision Stump
- M5
- Conditional Decision Trees

Bayesian Algorithms

These methods are known as Bayesian methods as they explicitly apply Bayes' Theorem for various problems that include classification and regression.

The most common Bayesian algorithms are:

- Naive Bayes
- Gaussian Naive Bayes
- Multinomial Naive Bayes
- Averaged One-Dependence Estimators (AODE)
- Bayesian Belief Network (BBN)
- Bayesian Network (BN)

Clustering Algorithms

These are like regression as they describe the class of problem as well as the class of methods. Different modeling approaches organize them, for instance, centroid-based and hierarchal. All of these use the inbuilt structures in the data for a better organization of the data into small groups of maximum commonality.

Following are the highly popular clustering algorithms:

- K-Means
- K-Medians
- Expectation Maximization (EM)
- Hierarchical Clustering

Association Rule Learning Algorithms

It identifies the rules that evaluate the relationships between data and variables. These rules can find many commercially useful and relevant associations in massive and multidimensional data sets. These can be used with organizations.

Some examples include:

- Apriori algorithm
- Eclat algorithm

Artificial Neural Network Algorithms

These are networks that have been modeled and inspired by the functioning and structures of the biological nerves. They are often used for classification problems as well as regression, but it may encompass various other things, as it is a huge field with various epistemological fields and sides.

Highly popular artificial neural network algorithms include:

- Perceptron
- Back-Propagation
- Hopfield Network
- Radial Basis Function Network (RBFN)
- Deep Learning Algorithms

Deep Learning Algorithms

These are modern and highly up to date artificial neural networks that can use cheap and abundant computation. You will find more about these in the following chapters. These concern with the construction of large as well as highly complex networks of neurons.

Some of the most popular deep learning algorithms include:

- Deep Boltzmann Machine (DBM)
- Deep Belief Networks (DBN)

- Convolutional Neural Network (CNN)
- Stacked Auto-Encoders
- Dimensionality Reduction Algorithms

Dimensional Reduction Algorithms

These are like clustering methods, and they try to find and use the inbuilt structure of the data. In these cases, this is done in an unsupervised manner.

This can be useful to visualize dimensional data or to simplify data that can then be used in a supervised learning method.

Ensemble Algorithms

These models are made of various weaker models that have been trained independently to work on specific tasks. The predictions of all these models are then combined to form an ensemble prediction. A lot of effort is put into the types of weak learners as well as how they can be combined. It is supposed to be a highly powerful technique.

Chapter 4: Decision Tree and Random Forests: Part One

This and the following two chapters will deal with the primary subject matter of this books i.e. decision trees and random forests. As decision trees and random forests is a vast field, it has been broken down into three chapters for the ease of the reader, so that even if the reader is a beginner or an amateur, they would be able to follow the information in the book. Let us now begin with the basics of decision trees.

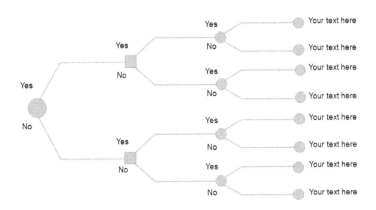

What is a Decision Tree? How exactly does it work?

Before beginning any topic, it is necessary to understand the basics of it and what it entitles. Thus, this section will deal with general information regarding Decision Trees.

In simple language a Decision Tree can be defined as a kind or type of learning algorithm that is supervised and has a pre-defined target variable that is commonly used in classification problems. Classification problems are a forte of Decision Trees as they fit perfectly with classification problems.

Decision trees can be used in both continuous input output variables as well as categorical output variables. In this method, the sample is split into two or more homogeneous sets by most significant splitter or differentiator in input variables.

Example:

Let's take a look at a sample of 30 children with three different variables viz. Gender (M or F), Town (A or B) and Weight (50 to 60 kg). 15 of these 30 play piano in their free time. Now, the condition is that I want to create a model that will predict who plays piano in their free time.

For this problem, it is necessary to differentiate the children and add them in categories such as children who play the piano. This should be based on highly significant input variable in between all the three.

In such a case a decision tree can help a lot as it differentiates and categorizes children using all the all the three variables and will form the most homogenous groups of students that will be heterogeneous to each other.

Decision Tree, Algorithms

Decision trees, as mentioned above finds and identifies the most significant variable as well as its value. This finds the best homogeneous set of data. However, the question that comes out of this is how does it do this, i.e. how does it identify the variable as well as the split. The decision tree uses a variety of algorithms to perform this action. These algorithms will be discussed in the next few sections of this chapter.

Types of Decision Trees

The categorization of the decision tree can be based on the kind of target variable that is available. It is found that it can be of two types:

Categorical Variable Decision Tree:

A Decision Tree that has categorical target variable is known as a categorical variable decision tree. For instance: If we are to continue the above example. The target variable in it will be "Children play piano or not." i.e. YES or NO.

Continuous Variable Decision Tree:

This is the second type of decision tree. If the tree has an ongoing target variable, it is known as Continuous Variable Decision Tree.

Example: Instead of continuing the above example, let us try something different. Let's assume that a person will pay his tax to the tax department (Yes/No). Here it is seen that the income of the individual is the important variable. However, the tax company may or may not have the details of the person. Now, as we already are aware of the importance of the variable, a decision tree can be constructed to predict the income using variables like the product, occupation, etc. In such a case the predictions are happening for a continuous variable.

Terminology and Jargon related to Decision Trees

As machine learning is a complicated and complex topic, it has its language that is full of jargon. Similarly, the field of Decision Tree too has its jargon that is often full of tree metaphors. Let us have a look at the most important idioms.

- Root Node: It stands for the total sample or population. It is then further divided into two or more homogeneous sets.
- Splitting: This is the process that is used to classify nodes into two or more sub-nodes.
- Decision Node: The further division of sub-nodes into more sub-nodes is also

known as splitting. However, the node created in this process is known as a decision node.

- Leaf/ Terminal Node: The Nodes that cannot be split are known as Leaf or Terminal node.

- Pruning: Continuing the metaphors of tree and plants, the process in which the subnodes of a decision node are removed, is known as pruning. It is thus an anti-splitting process.

- Branch / Sub-Tree: As the name suggests, the sub-section of a complete tree is known as a sub-tree or branch.

- Parent and Child Node: In the division of the nodes, the node that gets divided is referred as a parent node, while the nodes that are formed due to this division, i.e. the sub-nodes are known as child nodes.

These are the most commonly used jargons in the Decision Tree terminology. Now let us have a look at the advantages and disadvantages of the algorithm.

There exists no perfect machine-learning algorithm, and all algorithms have one problem or the other. Hence, instead of criticizing an algorithm, it is necessary to study its advantages and disadvantages and use it according to your requirements and needs. Below you will find the pros and cons of decision tree algorithm discussed in brief.

Advantages

Easy to understand:
Even for the people who do not have an analytical background, decision tree algorithm is very easy to comprehend. A user does not need to have any statistical knowledge or information to study, read and interpret the trees. Users can easily read the data in decision trees, as the graphical representation is highly intuitive and user-friendly.

It is believed that decision tree, if not the fastest, then definitely one of the fastest method of identification of the most significant variable as well as the relation between two or more than two variables. A decision tree can help users to create new variables as well as features. These new features will have more strength for predicting the target variable. It is also usable in the data exploration stage. For instance, let's say the user is working on a project where the data is available in the form of multiple variables. Here the decision tree will work and predict the most significant variable with ease.

As said in the first chapter, in machine learning, a user has to spend most of their time in data cleaning and separating the good data from the bad data. However, in the case of the decision tree, this process is considerably easy and does not take a lot of time. It remains uninfluenced by the missing values as well as outliers, and thus the cleaning process becomes straightforward.

The data type is not a constraint:
Decision tree is a versatile algorithm, and it can handle categorical as well as numerical data variables with ease.

Non-Parametric Method:
A nonparametric method means a method that has no assumptions regarding classifier structures or spatial distribution. A decision tree is a non-parametric method.

Disadvantages

Over fitting:
Decision tree models have many difficulties out of which over fitting is the most common and practical. However, this problem can be solved with using constraints on model parameters as well as pruning. An example is discussed in the following section.

Although it can work with continuous variables, it is not at all suitable for it. Decision tree starts losing information when it starts categorizing variables in more and more categories.

Regression Trees vs. Classification Trees

The last stage in a decision tree is the terminal nodes that are also known as the leaves. What this means is that the decision trees are normally constructed upside down, where the leaves are at the bottom while the roots are at the top.

The above-mentioned trees, both work in similar or almost similar ways, however there exist some minor differences that are quite important. Let us go through them one by one.

When the dependent variable is continuous, the regression trees are used whereas when the dependent variable is categorical; the classification trees are used.

The value gained by the terminal nodes in the sample data is the mean of response observed in the case of a regression tree. Therefore, in the case of data observation, its prediction is the mean value.

Whereas, the class gained by the terminal node in the sample data is the mode of observation in the case of the classification tree. Therefore, if some unseen data comes under that region the prediction that takes place the mode value.

Both the types of trees separate the predictor space in different, non-overlapping spaces. They are in a way, high- dimensional boxes.

Both trees use a top-down greedy method. This approach is known as recursive binary splitting. It is a top-down method as it starts from the top of the tree, where the observations are present in a single region and then divides the predictor space into two new branches down the tree. It is said to be 'greedy' as, the algorithm that looks for a best available variable in only the current split. It does not concern about the future splits that lead to a superior tree. The splitting or dividing process goes on until the stopping criterion defined by the user is achieved. For instance: the user can order the algorithm to stop as soon as the number of observations in each node goes below than 50.

In such cases, the dividing process or the splitting process gives an output of fully constructed or grown trees until the criterion is reached. However, it is most likely that the data will over-fit the tree. This leads to a bad accuracy in the form of unseen data. Due to this, pruning is necessary. It is normally used for solving the problem of over-fitting. More on this in the next section!

Where does the tree get split?

Where should the tree get split is an important question that all the users ask. This decision often affects the trees' accuracy by a large margin. However, the criteria that are used to make this decision are different in the case of classification and regression trees.

Multiple algorithms are used by the decision trees to make decisions where to split and how much to split. There is an increase in the homogeneity when the sub-nodes are created. This means that the purity of the nodes is enhanced when the target variable increases.

The selection of algorithm is also based on the kind of target variables. The four, most commonly used algorithms in such decision trees are:

Gini Index

In Gini Index, if two items are selected from a population, randomly, then they need to be of the same class. The probability for this will be one of the population will be pure.

- It will work with the categorical target variable such as "Success" or "Failure."
- It can only do Binary splits.
- The more the value of Gini, the more the value of homogeneity.
- Gini method is used to do binary splits by the CART (Classification and Regression Tree).

Let us look at the steps that can be used to calculate by Gini for a split:

The following formula is used to calculate the Gini for the subnodes

Sum of square of probability for success and failure i.e. (p^2+q^2)

Now calculate the Gini for the division for weighted Gini of each node of the created split.

For instance: In our first example, where we need to segregate the children on the basis of target variable i.e. playing piano or not.

Calculate, Gini for sub-node Female = $(0.2)*(0.2) + (0.8)*(0.8) = 0.68$

Gini for sub-node Male = $(0.65)*(0.65) + (0.35)*(0.35) = 0.55$

Calculate weighted Gini for Split Gender = $(10/30)*0.68 + (20/30)*0.55 = 0.59$

Gini for sub-node Class IX = $(0.43)*(0.43) + (0.57)*(0.57) = 0.51$

Gini for sub-node Class X = $(0.56)*(0.56) + (0.44)*(0.44) = 0.51$

Calculate weighted Gini for Split Class = $(14/30)*0.51 + (16/30)*0.51 = 0.51$

Above, you can see that Gini score for Split on Gender is higher than Split on Class, hence, the node split will take place on Gender.

Chi-Square

This algorithm is used to find the statistical significance of the differences between the parent node and the sub-node. We can calculate it by the sum of all the squares of all the differences between the expected frequencies of target variable and observed frequencies of the target variable.

Categorical target variable "Success" or "Failure" are used.

It can perform two or more than two splits.

The more the value of Chi-Square the higher is the value of the statistical significance of differences between the parent node and the sub-node.

The following formula is used to calculate the Chi-Square of each node:

Chi-square = $((Actual - Expected)^2 / Expected)^{1/2}$

The formula forms a tree that is known as CHAID (Chi-square Automatic Interaction Detector)

Necessary steps to undertake to calculate Chi-square for a split:

The Chi-square for an individual node is to be calculated by calculating the deviation for 'Success' as well as 'Failure' both.

The resultant Chi-square are then added and summed to calculate the ultimate Chi-square.

Information Gain, Decision Tree

Now it is possible to construct a conclusion that a low amount of impure nodes need less information to describe them. This information theory is used to measure and define the degree of disorganization in a system. This is known as Entropy. For instance, if a sample is 100%

homogeneous then the entropy level is zero, however, if the sample is divided equally then the entropy level is 1 or one.

The lesser the entropy, the better it is.

Calculate and formulate the entropy of parent node.

Formulate the entropy of each separate node in the split and then calculate the average weighted of all the other nodes that are present in the split.

Reduction in Variance

Until now we have seen the algorithms for target variables. When the variance is reduced, it is an algorithm that can be used in continuous target variables. This algorithm utilizes standard formula of variance that can be used to choose the best split.

How to calculate Variance:
Formulate the variance for each node.

Formulate the variance for every split as a weighted average of every node variance.

Till now we have seen the basics of decision trees as well as the basics of decision-making process that chooses the best splits for a tree model. This tree can be used and applied to both classification problems and regression problems.

How to avoid over-fitting in trees and what are the main parameters in tree modeling?

Over-fitting is one of the major problems that researchers face when constructing decision trees. If a limit does not exist in a decision tree, then it presents you 100% accuracy. However, in the worse case scenario, it will construct one leaf for every observation. Thus, it becomes extremely important to avoid over-fitting while constructing a decision tree. This can be done using the following two methods:

- Setting constraints on tree size
- Tree pruning

Let us discuss the first one in brief.

How to set Constraints on Tree Size

This can be performed using a variety of parameters that can be used to define a tree.

These parameters are explained below. These are irrespective of the tool used. These parameters are available in R as well as Python.

- Minimum Samples for a node split.
- It can define a number of observations that are needed for a required node for splitting.
- It is also used to limit over-fitting. A large number of values can prevent learning relations.
- A large number of values can also lead to under-fitting.
- It can define the minimum sample for a leaf.
- It can be used to control over-fitting.
- Lower values are appreciated for the imbalanced class problems, as the

regions in which minority class turns out to be majority class are minuscule.

Maximum Depth of Tree:

- This can be used to check the depth of a tree.
- It is used to control over-fitting.
- It needs to be tuned using CV.
- It has a large number of terminal nodes.

Chapter 5: Decision Trees: Part 2

In this chapter certain topics such as tree pruning, etc. will be handled.

Tree Pruning

As mentioned in the last chapter, the method of setting a constraint is considered to be a greedy-approach, and thus, it is not recommended. What this means is that the method will just check for the best split and more on forward until one of the many given stopping conditions are achieved. For, instance if we are to use the metaphors of driving then:

Let us assume that there are two lanes.

In lane one, cars are moving at 90km/h.

In lane two, trucks are moving at 40km/h.

You are driving a red car, and now you have two options. You can either take a left turn and overtake the two cars that are driving in front of you, as soon as possible, or continue to be in your lane.

Let us now go through these choices one by one. In the choice number one, you will take over the cars immediately and then move into a lane where the trucks are driving. Now you will have to drive in the lane with the trucks at the speed of 40km/h until a spot opens up in the old lane. Meanwhile, the cars in the original lane, which were behind you, have moved on and gone ahead of you. Your choice would be the best choice if your mission were to cover the most distance in around 20 seconds. However, in the latter choice, you will continue with your speed, cross the trucks and then get a chance to take over and go ahead.

This is the difference between pruning and normal decision tree. A decision tree that has constraints will not be able to see the 'truck' or the obstruction in front of it and will try to take a greedy approach. However, if pruning is used, the method will take a few steps back and will get a chance to think upon the condition before acting on it.

This means that pruning is better than the other option. So how to use it?

For utilizing pruning, it is necessary to make decision tree with a large depth.

Then we need to begin at the bottom and then slowly and gradually start cutting off the leaves that are presenting negative results as compared from the top.

For instance, if a split is giving a result of -10 i.e. the loss of 10, then in the subsequent split should give us a gain of 20.

A simple decision tree will halt its working at step one, however, after pruning, we will begin to see the overall gain rising to +10 all the while keeping both the leaves.

Linear models or tree based models?

The use of the algorithm is dependent on the type of problem that you are trying to solve. Let us have a look at some factors that you need to consider and that can help you decide the algorithm that is to be used when solving a problem:

If the relationship between independent and dependent variable is approximated using a linear model, the linear regression will outperform the model.

If there exists a high nonlinearity as well as the complex relationship between the independent & dependent variables, a tree model will serve better than a regular method.

A decision table is a much easy to understand and explain model as compared to a linear model.

Ensemble methods:

The dictionary meaning of the word ensemble is a group. Thus, ensemble methods are made of a group of predictive models that can gain better stability and accuracy. They are also known to boost the tree-based models.

Like all other models that we have seen by now, a decision tree based model too has certain problems. These problems include bias and variance. Here bias stands for the difference between the average values that predicted than the actual values. Variance refers to the variety of the predictions of models at the same point if the samples are taken from one same population.

When the complexity of the model is increased, it is possible to see the reduction in the prediction error thanks to lower bias in the model. However, when you gradually continue to build a more complicated model you can over-fit your model, and thus your model may suffer from the high variance.

A strong and highly powerful model should be able to maintain a proper balance between the above-mentioned types of errors. This is also known as the trade-off management of bias-variance errors. One of the best ways to do the tradeoff analysis is to perform ensemble learning.

The most common methods of ensemble learning are as follows:

- Bagging
- Boosting
- Stacking

In this chapter, we'll focus on Bagging in detail while Boosting will be handled in the next chapter.

What is bagging? How does it work?

Bagging is a method that is used to decrease the variance of the predictions by summing the output of two or more classifiers that are modeled on different samples in the same data set.

The following steps are followed in bagging:

Create Multiple Data sets:
The original data is replaced in sampling with the formation of new data sets.

The new data sets may contain fractions of the rows and columns. These are normally hyper parameters in a bagging model.

If the columns and rows are taken in the fraction that is less than one, it can help to make the model strong and robust. It can also reduce over-fitting.

Build Multiple Classifiers:
These are constructed with each new data set.

Normally the same classifier is constructed on every data set, and the predictions are made later.

Combine Classifiers:
All the predictions of every classifier are combined with the help of a mode, a mean or a median. This depends on the problem on the hand.

The combined values are normally stronger than a single value.

It is important to notice that the number of models that are to be constructed here is not supposed to be a hyper parameter. A greater number of models are almost always better than lower numbers. However, in certain cases, they can also perform on similar planes and thus can give a similar performance to the lower numbers. It is possible to show this theoretically that the variance of all the combined predictions are reduced to 1/n where n is the number of classifiers, of the normal variance under certain assumptions.

A variety of implementations of bagging models exist. Random forest is one of such models. It will be discussed it in the next and the last chapter of the decision tree series.

Chapter 6: Decision Trees: Part Three (Random Forests)

In this chapter let us focus on the basics of Random Forests and how it performs its tasks. Random Forest can be called as a universal solution as it is said if you do not know which algorithm to use, you should use a random forest.

The random forest can be defined as a versatile and smart machine learning method that can perform both classifications as well as regression tasks. It can also perform dimensional reduction methods, outlier values, treat missing values and other steps of data exploration as well. It is an expert solution for most of the problems. It is known as an ensemble way of learning as a group of weak models are combined to form this, powerful model.

Workings of Random Forest:

Multiple decision trees are grown in a random forest. This is opposite to the CART model. For the classification of new object based attributes, every one of the trees presents a classification. This presentation is also known as 'voting' for the class. The forest then is given a choice to choose the classification with the most votes.

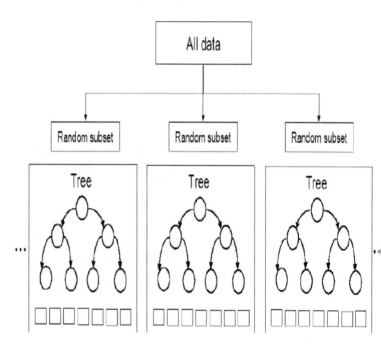

For instance:

Let's say that the number of cases in one training set is N. Then the sample of the N cases can be taken at random. However, it must be replaced. The sample will serve as the training set for the growing tree.

If there exist M input variables then, m<M is specified in a way that at each node, the m variables will be selected at random out of the M. The split will happen on M and m is used to split node.

All the trees are grown as much as they can grow, and no pruning is done.

The prediction of new data takes place by aggregating the other predictions of the ntree.

Advantages of Random Forest

- Random forest algorithm can be used in both sorts of problems. It can be used in regression as well as classification.

- It can handle a large amount of data set in high dimensionality. It can handle more than a few thousands of variables and can very well identify the significant ones among them. It is therefore considered to be an important dimensionality reduction method.

- It can effectively estimate the missing data and can easily maintain accuracy even if it is fed a large amount of data.

- It has various methods that can be used to balance errors in the data set.

- The above features can be used with unlabeled data as well. Thus, it can work unsupervised.

- It samples input data with replacement. This process is known as bootstrap sampling.

Disadvantages of Random Forest

- Like advantages, Random Forest has certain disadvantages too. However, as compared to the disadvantages, the number of advantages is large, thus making Random forests a far better option than other options.

- It is not as good at regression as it is with classification. It often does not come out with precise, continuous nature predictions. It cannot make predictions beyond the range of the provided training data in the case of regression.

- The data may become over-fit if the sample data is too noisy.

- It can act as a black box approach for statistical modelers as you cannot control the performance of the model. You can only try random seeds and different parameters.

What is Boosting? How does it work?

To define in simple terms, boosting is a family of algorithms that transform weak learners to strong or stronger learners.

The definition can be further understood by the use of the following example that deals with spam email identification:

If you are asked to identify Spam and regular mail, what will be the criteria that you will follow to perform your task? Normally, the following steps will be followed:

- If the email contains only one, promotional image: SPAM
- It only has link or links: SPAM
- The body of the email contains only sentences such as "You won a prize money of ---": SPAM
- Email received from an official domain: Not a SPAM
- Email received from a known sender: Not a SPAM

Thus, these are the rules or the criteria that we use to classify whether an email is a spam or not spam. However, do you firmly believe that these criteria are sufficient enough to classify emails in spam and not spam? The answer to the above question is no.

These rules cannot be said to be powerful enough to classify email as spam or not spam on their own. Hence, these rules are known as a weak learner. However, these weak learners can be converted into strong ones by combining the predictions made by the weak learners with the help of various methods such as:

By utilizing average or weighted average Choosing the prediction that has a higher vote rate.

For instance: In the above example we have five weak learners. If three out of these five are said to be SPAM, then the remaining two will be voted as Not Spam. Therefore, we will continue to consider an email SPAM because the votes are higher in the case.

How does it work?

As we have seen that boosting actually sums the weak learners to form a strong rule. However, the question that should arise in your mind is, how does it identify the weak rules?

To find the weak rule it is necessary to apply the machine-learning algorithm with a varied distribution first. Every time this algorithm is applied, a new weak prediction rule is formed. This is a repetitive process and is repeated many times. The boosting algorithm combines these rules into one single strong prediction rule.

How do we choose a different distribution for each round?

To choose the correct distribution, the following steps can be followed:

1.   All the distributions are taken and assigned by the base learner to equal weight and attention.

2.   If any prediction error happens due to the first base learning algorithm, more

attention is then paid to the observation that has caused the error. It is then applied to the next base-learning algorithm.

3. The second step is repeated until the base learning algorithm limit is reached or a high level of accuracy is gained.

In the last step, it sums up all the results received from the weak learners and makes a strong learner. This learner can improve the prediction power of the model eventually. Boosting is highly focused on mis-classified and high error examples that are preceded by weak rules.

Many boosting algorithms exist that can enhance the accuracy of boosting models even more. Following is a tutorial where you can learn even more about the two most commonly used boosting methods: Gradient Boosting (GBM) and XGBoost.

GBM or XGBoost: Which is more powerful?

Many researchers have admired the boosting capabilities of XGBoost. It often gives out a better output as compared to GBM however, in many cases it is seen that the benefits are less, often inconsequential. XGBoost is better than GBM for the following reasons:

Regularization:

XGBoost has regularization, unlike Standard GBM implementation that has no regularization. Regularization can control the amount of over-fitting. This is why the other name for XGBoost is 'regularized boosting technique.'

Parallel Processing:

Unlike GBM XGBoost has parallel processing, which makes it considerably faster than regular boosting.

A question that might arise in your mind is that how boosting, a serialized or sequential process can be parallelized? This can be explained by the following simple clarification. A decision tree can only be constructed on the base of an older one or a previous one. Hence, it is possible to create or grow a new tree from each core. Thus, it is a versatile method.

XGBoost can also work with Hadoop.

High Flexibility

XGBoost is far more flexible than GBM as it allows the user to optimize and personalize whatever evaluation criteria ass well as optimization objectives that the user wants to change. This makes it highly powerful as it practically removes the limitations from the field and it possible to do whatever you want.

XGBoost is a better option than GBM because it can handle missing values better than GMB. The user can supply a different value that is not the observation and can pass it as a parameter. XGBoost will try to perform different tasks as it can locate a missing value on every node and can learn the path as well.

Tree Pruning:

A GBM often stops splitting nodes when it locates a negative loss in the split. Therefore, it is considered to be a greedier algorithm. Compared to GBM, XGBoost can split till the max_depth of the value is achieved and then it starts the pruning mechanism where it removes the splits, going backward when it cannot find a positive gain.

Built-in Cross-Validation

XGBoost has a built in mechanism of cross-validation that is run at the each repetition. Thus, it becomes extremely easy to derive the perfect number of boosting repetitions in a single run. This is not seen in the case of GBM where you have to run a grid-search, and only some specific values get tested in the mechanism.

Continuing the Existing Model

It possible to start the XGBoost model from any last iteration in the last run. This is highly important in certain applications.

How to work with GBM in R and Python?

It is necessary to understand the necessary parameters before we have a look at the algorithm itself. These can be used in R as well as Python.

Following is the pseudo-code of GBM algorithm for two classes:

Start the outcome.

1. Repeat from 1 to the actual number of trees.
2. Add the weights for the targets after each run. These will be based on the previous run itself.
2.1. Fix the model on the selected data subsample.
2.2. Perform predictions till a full set of observation is done.
2.3. Update the results with the current results. Identify the learning rate.
3. Return the last output.

Although this is a basic and very naïve explanation of GBM, yet it will help the beginners to understand the workings of the algorithm.

Now let us have a look at the parameters that are used in Python:

learning_rate

This identifies the impact of every single tree on the final result. GBM begins the work by initializing the starting estimate. This is then updated with the help of result of all the subsequent trees. The learning parameter is used to control the magnitude of the change that is seen in the estimates.

In this example, lower values are more appreciated as they can make the model stronger to certain characteristics of the tree. This allows them to generalize well.

n_estimators

This stands for the number of sequential trees that need to be modeled. GBM is quite robust at a large number of trees. However, it may over-fit at a certain point. Hence, this parameter is used to tune the learning rate.

Subsample

This is the fraction of observations that are to be chosen for every tree. This is performed using random sampling.

Values that are less than 1 can make the model strong by slowing down the variance. Generally, values of ~0.8 used and work great.

Apart from the above mentioned, there are certainly other parameters that can be used to enhance the performance of the method.

Loss

It is in reference to the loss function. This is to be minimized with each split.

This parameter can have many values for both, regression and classification. Normally the default values are used. Other values are to be used only if you understand their role.

Init

This parameter affects the initialization of the output. It can be used if another model whose result is to be used as the initial estimates for GBM has been constructed.

random state

This is the random number seed due to which the same random numbers get generated whenever they are used.

This parameter is necessary for tuning. If a random number is not fixed, then we cannot have different results for all the following runs on the same parameters. This makes it difficult to compare the models.

Verbose

This refers to the type of output that is to be printed when the model fits well. The values can be varied, and they are as follows:

1. 0: No sort of result is generated. This is the default value.
2. 1: Result is generated at only certain intervals for the trees.

3. >1: Result is generated for all the trees.

This is an interesting parameter, and it can help the user in a significant way if it is used judicially and properly. This parameter can be used to fit extra trees on the previous models with ease. This will allow you to save a lot of time and thus allow you to conduct various advanced applications.

This is used when you need to choose whether to presort the data for quicker splits. It creates an automatic selection by default. However, the values can be changed if necessary.

For R users who use caret package these are the main tuning parameters:

- N.trees – This is the number of repetitions and the tree that will be used to grow the subsequent trees.
- Interaction.depth – It identifies the complexity of the tree or the total

number of splits that the tree has to perform.

- Shrinkage – This is used in the reference of learning rate. It similar to the learning rate as presented in python.
- N.minobsinnode – It is the minimum number of training samples that are needed for a node to continue splitting.

Where to practice?

To master any skill or concept, it is necessary to practice regularly. Similarly, you also need to practice regularly if you want to master the above-mentioned algorithms.

Practicing is easy for the above-mentioned algorithms as there are many online services where you can find practice games and tests. These tests are updated frequently, and you can also participate in a variety of competitions that can help you master algorithms. These competitions often feature a global level leaderboard, so not only can you practice your algorithms, but also can show off your skills and progress to the whole world. You can also find offline practice sets that can be used to practice when you cannot connect to the Internet.

Thus, here ends the three part series of Decision Tree learning series in this book. In the next chapter, let us have a look at some other forms of machine learning that becoming highly popular in today's world.

Chapter 7: Deep Learning

Till now we have discussed the basics of machine learning and the basics and working so f decision trees and random forests as well. However, it is clear that the field of machine learning does not end here; rather it grows in size as well as complications hereafter. One of the major concepts that are becoming highly popular nowadays is Deep learning. This chapter will serve as a minor introduction to this method of learning.

Deep learning or hierarchical learning is said to be the use of non-biological neural networks to study and learn the aspects that have one or more than one hidden layers. It is situated in the learning data representations. In the method, the learning can be totally supervised, partially supervised or not supervised at all.

The architectures of deep belief system, deep learning system, recurrent neural networks as well as deep neural networks all are used and applied in many fields including computer vision, speech recognition, machine translation, social network filtering, natural language processing, bioinformatics, sound recognition, etc. Here these methods give out outputs that can easily compete with the results that are given out by human users.

Deep learning thus is a family or class of machine learning algorithm that uses a cascade of more than two layers of nonlinear processing units for feature extraction and transformation. These layers are cascading and nested therefore the output, or the result of the last layer becomes the input or the sample for the next or following layer. These can be supervised or unsupervised, ex- classification and pattern analysis. The unsupervised ones use multifaceted levels of data. They also use the representations of the data. The method is nested here where the higher level features are based on, the lower level features.

The World School Council of London first designed deep learning.

The main difference or rather the main characteristic difference between the above-mentioned three concepts is that Deep learning is a type of machine learning whereas machine learning is a form of AI or artificial intelligence. Machine learning is considered to be the most popular approaches or forms of artificial intelligence. However, not all of the systems based on AI use machine learning, for instance, self-driven or automatic cars use rule-based systems.

It has been prophesized that in the coming future machine learning will be the most prominent form of AI.

Deep learning can be defined as a type or kind of approach towards machine learning that is extremely popular and advanced.

Though the future of machine learning is bright, however, it is not concrete. If another technique is invented that turns out to be better than machine learning, it will be replaced as soon as possible, without any issue.

Chapter 8: Digital Neural Network and Computer Science

(Enlarged Legend)

The modern computer and computing were invented in the 20th century. People everywhere have guessed and tried to speculate the achievements and innovations that the computers might create in the future. Some of them include talking to humans, recognizing their faces as well as gestures, playing games such as chess against humans, driving cars, etc. It is to be noted that computers have and are still performing all the above-mentioned activities. Most of these are due to the development and growth of AI and machine learning, especially in the case of Digital Neural Network.

Deep learning is a form of sophisticated and highly developed form of neural networks. These were first developed and used about 70 years ago. Two scientists, Walter Pitts and Warren McCullough in 1944, first thought of the idea. However, the research soon changed its trajectory, and it stopped developing.

However, in the 90s it rose again, and now it is considered to be the most important concept in the AI.

Artificial neural networks are also known as ANN are computing systems that are based on biological neural networks commonly seen in the brains of animals, especially animals. Thus, it is an imitation of the intricate system of neurons that have been developed by nature.

The best feature of this system is that it learns and performs tasks by inspecting examples without the need of task-specific programming. This thus decreases the time as well as the resources that are required.

An ANN group is constructed of multiple artificial neurons. These are connected with each other where the connections are used to transmit and transfer signals from one neuron to the other. They are also organized in multiple layers. Each of these layers performs a different and varied function. The signals normally travel many times through the whole set.

The biggest goal of ANN is the imitation of the human brain and the methods that are used by the human brain to solve these problems. However, nowadays the focus of ANN is changing and now it is more concentrated on the problem solving itself and not on imitating the neural networks. This is why scientists are coming up with many techniques and networks that are quite different than the natural ones but are far more powerful than the regular ones.

Applications of ANN

ANN is used in applications such as

- Solar energy to model and design better gadgets and appliances.
- Also used in system modeling.
- Can easily handle complicated and incomplete data.

- Can be used to solve nonlinear problems.
- Air conditioning systems
- Ventilation
- Refrigeration
- Heating
- Power Generation
- Load forecasting
- Estimation of heating loads in buildings and construction.
- Robotics
- Forecasting
- Pattern Recognition
- Medicine
- Manufacturing
- Social and psychological sciences
- Signal processing
- Optimization.
- Prediction of air flow
- Prediction of consumption of energy in a solar building.

Thus, it can be seen that artificial neural network can work wonders in the field of computers.

Advantages of ANN

- The neural network is able to perform tasks that cannot be performed by the linear network.
- As it is a nonlinear network, even if one or more elements fail, the network still continues to process and work.
- It need not be reprogrammed again and again.
- It is easy to use.
- It is an adaptive method of learning. It is highly robust and can solve a variety of difficult problems with relative ease. Can be used in a variety of applications.
- The advantages of ANN are far more than the disadvantages of risks that are associated with the technology.
- It uses simple samples to come up with results and responses.

- It is extremely flexible and adaptable. It can learn easily with very fewer variables.
- It is more forgiving to the user generated errors and thus is much more suitable than a linear network.
- Based on adaptive learning.

Risks associated with ANN

There are certain risks involved while using ANN. However, it can be seen that the list of advantages is much longer the list of risks:

- A user needs a lot of training to learn how to use ANN properly. However, once learned, it is quite easy to use.
- It is a time-consuming process.
- The architecture is different than microprocessor hence proper emulation is needed before using ANN.

Types of Artificial Neural Networks

Multiple types of ANN or artificial neural exists, out these, the following three are important.

- Feedback ANN: The result goes into the network itself, and the process gets repeated until the perfect result or output is achieved.
- Feed Forward ANN: It is a simple network. It contains an output layer, an input layer and one or more layer of neurons
- Classification Prediction ANN: It is a subset of the feed forward artificial neural network.

Summary:

The goal of AI (Artificial intelligence) is to mimic human capabilities, such as knowledge application, abstract thinking, reasoning, etc. On the contrary machine learning operates on the principles of using writing software based on past experiences.

To our surprise machine learning in actual fact is very similarly related to data mining and statistics as oppose to AI. Why is that? In essence when a computer program performs a particular task based on experiences from the past, than we can conclude the machine has "learnt". This is much different from a program performing a task as its' programmers have comprehensively defined its capacities already.

Machine learning can be placed into 3 distinct categories:

Supervised Learning - Teach and train machines with data that is already labeled with the correct answers and outcomes. The more data available the more the machine will learn from the given topic or subject matters. For instance, an apple is red, banana yellow , and broccoli is green. After the machine is trained it is given new unseen data and the learning algorithm uses its past experiences to determine an outcome.

Unsupervised Learning- when a machine is trained with data sets that do not have labels. The learning algorithm is not told what the data represents. So for example, here is a letter or an apple, but no further information is given on its details. Or perhaps describing characteristic of a certain object, like a tree, but not giving the label of its name.

So how does this work? Imagine listening to a podcast of a foreign language like Mandarin or Hindi. You listen to hundreds upon hundreds of podcasts and start to establish patterns, form models, and recognize certain sounds. - Unsupervised learning operates much in the same way.

Reinforcement Learning- similar to unsupervised learning, the data is not labeled. But when asked a question of the data, the outcome will be evaluated. So for instance, imagine playing against a computer in the game of chess.

When the computer wins it than evaluates the result to validate how it won and thus reinforces the action. Ergo, when the computer engages in playing thousands of games it collectively establishes a strategy and framework in winning.

There is this buzz word "Neural Net" we hear of in the world of machine learning, but what is it exactly? Its modeled after our brain neural networks and operates synonymously to a neuron. When a given number of inputs are given the neural will propagate a signal depending on how it interprets it.

The Above mentioned in this summary sub chapter is the fundamental concepts of machine learning. This is how machine learning functions and operates, and much of what we utilize today without even knowing it!

Conclusion

This is the era of technology, and thus it is changing and evolving every day. Every day, it is becoming extremely difficult to keep up with the new innovations, latest trends, discoveries and inventions in almost every field. This is especially true in the case of science and technology. Science and technology are the two fields that are developing the most rapidly in today's world. Hence, to keep up with such a never seen before pace, a person needs to be extremely up to date and techno-savvy. However, this not possible for everyone. Hence, books like this one help general population to understand the basics of the current buzzwords and concepts, so that they can be relevant. This book is an attempt to serve such population by helping them understand the basics of machine learning, AI, and decision trees in simple and lucid manner.

The book is best suited for beginners in who are interested in machine learning. However, you can also find information that is suitable for adepts as well. For the ease of the general reader, the language of the book has been kept simple and relatively jargon free. The book is divided into multiple sections so that you can only read the sections that are important for you.

The main concern of this book, tree based algorithms is highly important for all sort of scientists that deal with data. They are known to provide the best performing model as compared to other models in the machine learning family. In this book, different aspects of decision trees and random forests have been discussed. Tree based modeling has been discussed from scratch. I am sure that you must have learned the importance of decision tree and how a biological concept is being used to upgrade the technology.

I am sure that this book will act as a basic guide for everyone who is interested in AI. As stated earlier, it is written in a simple and lucid manner, so it suitable for every member of your family. As an added bonus, a few chapters have been dedicated to deep learning and neural networking. These will help as a guide if you want to study advanced machine learning. I also hope that this book has done away with any myths that you had about machine learning and AI.

 Once again thank you for buying this book and good luck!

If you enjoyed reading this book please leave a quality review on Amazon. It would be very helpful and appreciated. Link below...

LINK: http://amzn.to/2xCDN19

MARKO
MODE

SUPERVISED AND UNSUPERVISED MACHIN
MASTERING DATA SCIENCE & PY

Markov Models Supervised and Unsupervised Machine Learning:

Mastering Data Science & Python

Please consult a licensed professional before attempting any techniques outlined in this book.

By reading this document, the reader agrees that under no circumstances are is the author responsible for any losses, direct or indirect, which are incurred as a result of the use of information contained within this document, including, but not limited to, —errors, omissions, or inaccuracies.

Table of Contents

Introduction

In the following book, you will find a great deal of information on the mechanics of the Markov Model and how the model could be used in the world of machine learning though using the powerful yet simple language, Python. This book is for those who have just begun to study and understand Artificial Intelligence and Data Science.

Markov Models was discovered in the year 1916, by Andreevich Markov, a scientist who was studying and analyzing the frequency of different types of words in Pushkin's poems. Since then, the model created has been expanded to include representations of a number of probabilities like the Hidden Markov Model that is integral to our understanding and towards building artificial intelligence.

The structure of this book will define each section of the topic piece by piece. We will first take a look at Markov Models and the mathematical aspect of those models. We will then take a look at Hidden Markov Models (HMM) and also study the three problems of HMM and also identify the solutions to the same. After thoroughly investigating the Markov Models, we will look at different aspects of Machine Learning and look at Supervised and Unsupervised Machine learning in greater detail.

After understanding the concepts of Markov Models and Machine Learning, we will take a look at Artificial Intelligence and Data Science and understand certain aspects of them. We will then learn about how to apply these concepts in Python. Everything from installing

Python to programming a Markov Model in Python will be covered in detail.

At the end of the book, you will have a clear understanding of the mathematical aspects of Markov Models and Hidden Markov Models. You will also be able to build enough confidence to help you program Markov Models using Python.

Thank you for purchasing the book. I hope you find it helpful.

Markov Models

Chapter 1: Markov Models

Axioms to understand Markov Models

There are certain axioms that exist in probability and statistics that will need to be understood before looking at Markov Models.

Fundamental Axioms

Let us take a look at the various axioms that are used in Markov Models to understand the math that supports the model. One of the most fundamental axioms can be expressed as follows: $0 < P(A) < 1$

This states that the probability of any event occurring is always going to be greater than zero but less than one, both inclusive. This implies that the probability of the occurrence of any event can never be negative. This makes sense since the probabilities can never be more certain than hundred percent and least certain than zero percent.

Additive Property

The next axiom that is important to note can only be true when both events A and B are mutually exclusive.

$$P(A+B) = P(A) + P(B)$$

This axiom states that the probability of both events A and B occurring is the same as the sum of the individual probabilities of the events occurring if and only if both events exclude each other. For example, if A is the event that we get a six on rolling a die and B is the event that we get a five rolling a die, then this axiom holds. But, if B were assumed to be the event where we get an even number, this set would include the number six making the axiom false.

Joint Probability

This property can be expressed as follows:

$$P(a, b) = P(A=a, B=b)$$

This property can be read as the probability of a and b is the same as the probability that event A turns out in state 'a' and event B turns out in state 'b'.

Conditional Distribution Axiom

The conditional probabilities can be found using the following equation:

$$P\,(X{=}a \mid Y{=}b) = [P\,(X{=}a,\,Y{=}b)]\,/\,[P\,(Y{=}b)]$$

The equation above is read as, "The probability of the random variable X being a and the random variable Y being b is equal to the probability of X being a AND Y being b divided by the probability of Y being b".

The conditional distribution in statistics takes into account the probability that both events will occur given that one of the events has already occurred. The probabilities thus obtained are larger than the probability of the events X and Y occurring had Y not occurred earlier.

Chain Rule

The chain rule is important for one to understand before taking a look at Markov's

Model. This rule helps you obtain the joint probabilities of many variables with different properties. The equation can be expressed as follows:

$$P(a_1, a_2, a_3, ..., a_n) = P(a_1 \mid a_2, a_3, ... , a_n) * P(a_2 \mid a_1, a_3, ... , a_n) * .... P(a_{n-1} \mid a_n) * P(a_n)$$

This states that the probability of the occurrence of every event is equal to the probability that one event occurs given that every other event has already occurred multiplied throughout by the probability of the next event occurring given that the subsequent events have occurred and so on. This creates a chain of multipliers, which would need to be solved to obtain the probability for many events.

The Product Rule

There is a product rule that is based on the independence of events, which states that:

$$P(A, B) = P(A \mid B) * P(B) = P(B \mid A) * P(A)$$

This states that the probability of the occurrence of both events A and B is given by the probability of the occurrence of A assuming B has already followed, and multiplied with the probability of B. This is also equal to the probability of the occurrence of the event B given that A has already occurred multiplied by the probability of A. If you look closely at this equation, you will realize that this axiom simply multiplies the conditional distribution axiom with P(B) on both sides.

The independence of multiple probabilities can be confirmed using the following axiom:

$$P (X) = P (X \mid Y)$$

In simpler words, the probability of the event X occurring is equal to the probability of X occurring given that the event Y has already occurred. If this axiom were true, it would imply that the occurrence of the event Y does not affect the occurrence of event X because the probability of X is unchanged irrespective of what the probabilities of Y are.

Bayes' Rule

This rule is often used to identify the conditional probability when P (A, B) is not known. The equation used is as follows:

$$P (A|B) = [P (B|A)*P (A)]/P (B)$$

These various axioms are a great way to understand the logic behind Markov Models. Let us now take a look at the mathematical aspects of the Markov Model. As mentioned above, Markov Models was discovered in the year 1916 by Andreevich Markov, a scientist who was studying and analyzing the frequency of different types of words in Pushkin's poems. These models have now become an integral model to use while working with data science, artificial intelligence, and machine learning.

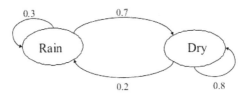

- Two states : 'Rain' and 'Dry'.
- Transition probabilities: $P(\text{'Rain'}|\text{'Rain'})=0.3$, $P(\text{'Dry'}|\text{'Rain'})=0.7$, $P(\text{'Ra'})=0.6$.
- in'|'Dry')=0.2, $P(\text{'Dry'}|\text{'Dry'})=0.8$
- Initial probabilities: say $P(\text{'Rain'})=0.4$, P('Dry

The Markov Property

In any system, the state of the system is constantly changing. This is the premise on which the Markov Models were developed. For any system to be a Markov model, it will also need to adhere to the Markov Property.

The property states that the past does not affect the future of any system, i.e. the next state of the system depends only on the current state of the system and only the single previous state affects the next state. For instance, if you were to consider the weather as a Markovian system, you can say for certain that if the weather was sunny yesterday and is humid today, the probability of it raining tomorrow would only depend on today.

Markov Models and Observation Probabilities

Before building a Markovian system, it is important to know the different states of the system. Let us consider an employee who is very sick. There are three states that he could be in – alive and healthy, sick and dead. We will then need to arrange all these states with their transition probabilities (probability of moving from one state to the next) in a matrix. The probabilities of moving from one state to another are identified and are calculated as the probability of being in one state at a particular time t+1.

Finally, it is important to understand the difference between state and observation. At times, you will be unable to tell what the weather is like outside when you are at work.

You will guess by what people are wearing. The observations that you make are what form the observation set. These observations are very different from the states since the states are definitive while observations are not.

Hidden Markov Model

Hidden Markov Model

The observational probability distribution that is obtained set of observations made is an integral part of the Hidden Markov Model. In a given Hidden Markov Model, the actual states are unknown to the observer implying that the observer can only make any observation of the effect of a given state. We have looked at an example of a person who is inside trying to make a decision on the weather outside. This could be the case in many circumstances. Hidden Markov Models are quintessential to machine learning for this reason. The variable that is in question is often not measurable or observable directly but can be measured by the effects it has on its surrounding environment. The probability of an observed state is called the emission probability.

Now let us take a look at the problems that the Markov Models and Hidden Markov Models cause – evaluation problem, decoding problem and learning problem. The evaluation problem looks at the likelihood of a sequence of observations considered, the decoding problem looks at the different states behind the observations made so far and the learning problem, the most complex problem determines the likely values for the events that may occur.

Chapter 2: Data Mining

Data mining is a process that is used by numerous businesses to convert the collected raw data into information that can be used by the business. There are specialized tools that can be used to detect patterns in large – scale information which would help you learn more about your consumers and also respond to their concerns while developing strategies that would help to increase your revenue. The ultimate goal of data mining is to increase your profits. Data mining is said to be effective only when data is gathered and stored in an efficient manner and processed in the right manner for future use.

Retail shops, like supermarkets and grocery stores, use data mining the most when compared with larger firms. There are a number of retailers offering loyalty rewards, which would motivate their customers to purchase only from that retail store since they would be able to reduce their expenditure. These rewards make it easier for the businesses to monitor who is purchasing what product, the time they purchase that product and also their usual budget. After conducting a thorough analysis, the retail store could choose to use the information obtained for different purposes, like providing customer coupons specifically targeted to their purchasing intent and deciding when to place items on sale or when to sell specific products at a higher markup.

Software

The software that is used for data mining is designed specifically to analyze the relationship within the data and the patterns that emerge from the data according to the needs of the business. For example, data mining software could be used to develop distinct classes of information. Let us take a look at how a grocery store could use data mining. The manager could use the software to understand when it would be the right time to hold a sale for a particular product. The software refers to the data that has been captured and will give the manager a clear idea on the customers' needs and likes. In some instances, data mining specialists may look for clusters of data according to logical relationships, or they study associations and patterns to make conclusions about consumer trends.

Strategies

There are different kinds of analysis that can be performed by businesses in order to obtain valuable data. There are different types of business data analytics that could be used to obtain different results each of which will impact the business differently. The type of strategy that needs to be used depends fully on the business and the kind of problem that the business is trying to address.

There are different forms of data analytics that could result in different outcomes thereby offering different insights on the data obtained by the business. One of the best ways to retrieve insights from data is through the process of data mining.

When it comes to developing the data analytics strategy, it is important to understand the definition of data mining and also understand how crucial it is to your business. It is important to take note that the goal of any data mining process is to look for relevant information that would be easily understood when looking at large scale data sets.

Below are the most common types of data mining analytics that you can use for your business.

Anomaly detection is the process of searching for information in a data set that does not match the expected behavior of the pattern that was predicted. Anomalies are also known as contaminants, exceptions, surprises and most commonly, outliers. They often offer information that is crucial. Outliers are certain parts of the data set that deviate considerably from the general average of the data set thereby causing a hindrance to the analysis. When looked at in numerical terms, these outliers are separate from the rest of the data and could signify that further analysis would need to be made to better understand the data.

Detecting anomalies in data sets could be used to identify if there are risks or frauds that are taking place within crucial systems. These outliers or anomalies have properties that would attract the attention of a data analyst who would then delve deeper to understand what is happening within the data set. This will help the business identify a number of crucial situations that indicate fraud, flaws in processes and also flaws in strategies used by the business.

It is important to take note that in large data sets, there are definitely going to be some anomalies. It is true that anomalies show bad data, but it is also true that these anomalies could be caused due to random variation and may not affect the data badly. In such situations, it is necessary to conduct more analysis.

Association Analysis

Association analysis helps the business identify the associations that exist between different variables in a large-scale data set. This strategy will allow the data analyst discover patterns that are concealed within the data which would help to identify variables inside the data and also understand the occurrences of some variables within the data set.

This strategy is commonly used in retail stores to identify patterns that are found within the data set or information from POS. These patterns can come in handy when it comes to identifying or recommending new products to other managers of the same retail store or to loyal customers based on what has been purchased before at the store. If you do this correctly, you will be able to increase your business's conversion rate and also increase your profits.

A good example would be that of Walmart's use of data mining since 2004. The retail giant discovered that the sale of Strawberry pops had increased by at least seven times before the hurricane. In response to this finding, the retail store placed this product at checkout counters when a hurricane was to strike in a particular area.

Regression Analysis

Regression analysis is used to determine the dependency, if any, between the different attributes in a data set. There is an assumption that one variable could elicit a response from another variable thereby causing a change in the data set.

Attributes that are often assumed to be independent could be affected by each other, which would mean that a dependency is created between them. By using regression analysis, the business owner will be able to identify if one variable is dependent on another variable and if there is any mutual dependency between the two.

A business can use regression analysis to identify and determine the levels of satisfaction of a client and how well this attribute can impact customer loyalty and also how the service could be affected.

Another good example to look at is the information collected by dating sites. They use regression analysis to offer better services to their users. For instance, if you have a Tinder account, the data provided by you is matched against the data provided by another member on tinder. If there is any dependency between these variables, you will find that person's profile on your feed.

Data mining could help businesses look for and focus on the most relevant and important information, which could be used to establish models that could help in making projections on how systems or people could behave so the business could make some projections.

When more data is gathered, better models can be built which would help you use the strategies in better ways resulting in a greater value for your business.

Clustering Analysis

The process of detecting data sets within data sets that have similar attributes is called clustering analysis. This type of analysis helps you identify the similarities and the differences between the data collected. Every cluster has a specific trait that would be used to enhance any algorithms that have been created by the business. For example, there could be customers who would often purchase the same products from the store and these customers could be grouped into a cluster. This cluster could be targeted and analyzed by the data analysts to increase the revenue for a firm.

An outcome of clustering analysis is the development of customer personas that can then be used to represent different customer types within a particular data set. This includes the behavior set or attitude of customers who are actually using the brands or products. The business can use a particular software or programming language to work on relevant cluster analysis.

Machine Learning

Chapter 3: What is Machine Learning?

It is not an easy task to define learning since it includes a wide range of processes. If one were to look into a dictionary for definitions of learning, one would come across phrases such as "to gain knowledge, or understanding of, or skill in, by study, instruction, or experience," and "modification of a behavioral tendency by experience." In a manner similar to the way psychologists study learning in humans, this book will focus on the learning processes of machines. Certainly, the two spheres of animal learning and machine learning are intertwined. A few techniques in machine learning are derived from some techniques used in the former. Also, breakthroughs in machine learning can help in bringing to light a few facets of biological learning.

When it comes to machines, speaking superficially, it can be said that any change to a machine's structure, data stored in memory or composition, in order to make the machine perform better and have better efficiency, can be the sign of learning in a machine. However, when we go deeper into the field, only a few of these changes can be subsumed into the category of machine learning. For instance, consider a machine that is meant to predict weather forecasts in a certain area for a few weeks. If data about the weather in the area over the past year is added to the memory of the machine, the machine can learn from this data and predict the weather more accurately. This instance can be called machine learning.

To be precise, the field of machine learning is applicable to machines that are associated with artificial intelligence. Machines associated with artificial intelligence are responsible for tasks such as prediction, diagnosis, recognition, and others. These types of machines "learn" from data that is added to them. This data is called training data because it is used to train the machine. The machines analyze patterns in this data and use these patterns to perform their actions. Machines use different learning mechanisms to analyze the data depending on the actions they are required to perform. These mechanisms can be classified into 2 broad categories- supervised learning and unsupervised learning.

Skeptics of the field of machine learning might question why machines need to learn in the first place. People may wonder why machines aren't designed specific to the tasks that they need to carry out. There are many reasons as to why machine learning is advantageous. As mentioned earlier, research into the field of machine learning can help us better understand certain aspects of human learning. Also, machine learning can also increase the accuracy and efficiency of machines. A few other reasons are:

- Even with the greatest efforts by engineers, some tasks cannot be defined explicitly. Some tasks need to be explained to the machine using examples. The idea is to train the machine with the input and teach it how to reach the output. This way, the machine will know how to deal with future inputs and process them to reach appropriate outputs.

- The field of machine learning is also intertwined with the field of data mining. Data mining is essentially the process of looking through loads and loads of data in order to find important correlations and relationships. This is another advantage of machine learning in that it might lead to the finding of important information.

- On many occasions, it is possible that humans design machines without correctly estimating the conditions in which it will be functioning. Surrounding conditions can play a huge role on the performance of the machine. In such cases, machine learning can help in the acclimation the machine to its environment so that the performance is not hindered. It is also possible that environmental changes might occur and machine learning will help the machine to adapt to these changes without losing out on performance.

- Another loophole in the process of human beings hardcoding the process into the machine is that the process might be extremely elaborate. In such a case, the programmer might miss out on a few details since it would be a very tedious job to encode all the details. So, it is much more desirable to allow the machine to learn such processes.

- There are constant changes in technology in the world. Major changes occur in other aspects as well such as vocabulary. Redesigning systems to accommodate for each and every change is not practical. Instead, machine-learning methods can be used in order to train the machines to adapt to these changes.

Subjects involved in machine learning

The sphere of machine learning is the intersection of many subjects. It derives information from a number of subjects. Each of these subjects brings in new methodology and terminology. All of these concepts come together to form the discipline of machine learning. Given below are a few of the subjects involved in machine learning.

Statistics

One of the most common problems in statistics that is used in machine learning is training, i.e. the usage of samples taken from an unknown probability distribution in order to predict what distribution a new sample is picked from. Another related problem is the estimation of the value of a function at a certain point based on the value of the function at a few sample points. Solutions to these problems are instances of machine learning because the problems involve estimation of future events based on data about past events. Statistics forms an extremely important part of machine learning.

Brain modeling

The part of brain modeling that is closely related to machine learning is the concept of neural networks. Scientists have suggested that one possible model for neurons or the neural network is non-linear components with weighted inputs. Extensive studies have been conducted on these non-linear elements in recent times. Scientists concerned with brain modeling are interested in gaining information about human learning from the study of these networks of neurons. Connectionism, sub-symbolic processing, and brain style computation are a few spheres that are associated with these types of studies.

Adaptive control theory

Control theory is a subject associated with the control of systems. A major problem faced by systems is the change in environmental conditions. Adaptive control theory is a part of this subject that deals with the methods by which systems can adapt to these changes and continue to perform optimally. The main idea is that the systems should anticipate these changes and modify themselves accordingly.

Psychological modeling

For many years now, psychologists have tried to understand the learning processes of humans. One such example is the EPAM network. This network was used for storing and retrieving one of two words when provided with the other. Later on, the concepts of decision trees and semantic networks were conceived in this field. In recent times, the work in the field of psychology has been strongly influenced by the subject of artificial intelligence. Another aspect of psychology that has been studied in recent times is reinforcement learning. This concept has also been used in machine learning extensively.

Artificial intelligence

As mentioned earlier, a large part of machine learning is concerned with the subject of artificial intelligence. Studies in artificial intelligence have focused on the usage of analogies for learning purposes and also on how past experiences can help in anticipating and accommodating future events. In recent years, studies have focused on devising rules for systems that use the concepts of inductive logic programming and decision tree methods.

Evolutionary models

It is a common idea in evolutionary studies that not only do animals learn to perform better in life, but they also learn to better adapt to their surroundings in order to enhance their performance. As far as machines are concerned, the concepts of learning and evolving can be considered to be synonymous with each other. Therefore, models that have been used to explain evolution can be used to devise machine-learning techniques. The most prominent technique that has been developed using evolutionary models is the genetic algorithm.

Varieties of Machine Learning

So far, this book has given an introduction to machine learning and has answered the question about the subjects that constitute it. Now, we come to the more important question of what can be learned in the subject of machine learning. The following are a few topics on which knowledge can be gained through the study of machine learning:

- Programs and logic rule sets
- Terminology and grammars
- Finite state machines
- Problem - solving systems
- Functions
- Artificial Intelligence
- Statistics

Out of the above, the two most focused on topics are those of statistics and artificial intelligence. These 2 subjects are used extensively in machine learning. We now move on to chapters that describe the two broad categories of machine learning techniques: supervised machine learning and unsupervised machine learning.

Uses of Machine Learning

Machine Learning is now a solution to complete manual tasks that are impossible to complete over a short span of time for a large amount of data. In this decade, we are overcome with data and information and have no manual way of processing this information paving a way for automated processes and machines to do that job for us.

Useful information can be derived when the process of analysis and discovery becomes automated. This will help us drive our future actions in an automated process. We have therefore come into the world of Big Data, Business Analytics, and Data Science. Predictive analytics and Business Intelligence are no longer just for the elite but also for small companies and businesses. This has given these small businesses a chance to participate in the process of collecting and utilizing information effectively.

Let us now take a look at some technical uses of machine learning and see how these uses can be applied to real world problems.

Density Estimation

This use of machine learning allows the system to use the data that is provided to create a product that looks similar to it. For instance, if you were to pick up the novel War and Peace from the shelves of a bookstore and run it through a machine, you will be able to make the machine determine the density of the words in the book and provide you with work that is exactly similar to War and Peace.

Latent Variables

When you work with latent variables, the machine uses the method of clustering to determine whether the variables are related to one another. This is a useful tool when you do not know what the cause of change in different variables is and also when you do not know the relationship between variables. Additionally, when the data set is large, it is better to look for latent variables since that helps to comprehend the data obtained.

Reduction of Dimensionality

Most often, data obtained has a number of variables and dimensions. If there are more than three dimensions, it is impossible for the human mind to visualize the data. It is in these instances that machine learning can help in reducing the data into a manageable number of dimensions so that the user understands the relationship between the variables easily.

Visualization

There are times when the user would just like to visualize the relationship that exists between variables or would like to obtain the summary of the data in a visual form. Machine learning assists in both these processes by summarizing the data for the user using specified or non-specified parameters.

Applications of Machine Learning in the Real World

There are three areas of knowledge where machine learning can be used effectively – business, web mining and scientific applications.

Business Applications

Machine learning can be used to profile customers, which would help businesses make better products that would cater to each segment of the customer base. Banks and other financial companies can detect frauds and can track the spending and saving patterns of customers to identify if there is something wrong with the account. For instance, in the TV Series 'Friends,' the credit card company called to confirm with Rachel if she was alright since she had not been using her card for some time. This will help companies retain their customers since they will begin to understand their customers better.

Businesses can also use machine learning to control and analyze the processes being used. For instance, businesses can track the amount of time spent by each sales executive over the phone and identify the sales that they have been able to make. Most businesses can use machine learning to understand their customers and also help to provide their customers with the right recommendations.

There are a number of different ways that unsupervised and supervised machine learning can be used by businesses, but these are often the most basic uses.

Web Mining

Machine learning is great for document searching and text mining. You can look for a particular object or organize all the information you have with respect to a particular object. Another example of supervised and unsupervised machine learning would be social media. Every social media platform keeps a track of the user's browsing and would provide the user with information or links that he or she would prefer to look at. The best example would be the recent update provided by Instagram where the platform would show the users the pictures that they would love the most at the top of their feed.

Machine learning can be used in a number of different applications right from genetics to pharmacology. In pharmacology, machine learning is used to identify and discover newer medicine and techniques to screen and prepare drugs. In medicine it is used to scan ECGs, MRIs and any other tests to identify any irregularities in the patterns obtained as a result of those tests. Machine learning can be used in satellite and probe data to understand the geological data that is obtained. Predictions can be made about any natural calamities that may occur using these data.

These applications of machine learning only graze the surface of the world of capabilities of machines to gather information. There are a number of other applications of machine learning which we are uncovering every single day.

Chapter4:Supervised Machine Learning

As mentioned earlier, an important process of machine learning is called training where the machine is fed with data about past events so that the machine can anticipate future events. When this training data is supervised, it is called supervised machine learning. The data fed essentially consists of training examples. These examples consist of inputs and the desired outputs. These desired outputs are also known as supervisory signals. The machine uses a supervised learning algorithm, which generates an inferred function used to forecast events. If the outputs are discrete, the function is called a classifier and if the outputs are continuous, the function is known as a regression function. This function is responsible for predicting outputs of future inputs. The algorithm needs to conceive a generalized method of reaching the output from the input based on the previous data. An analogy that can be made in the spheres of human and animal learning is concept learning.

Overview

Supervised learning is a method that uses a fixed algorithm. Given below are the steps involved in this algorithm:

1. The first and foremost step in supervised learning is the determination of the type of examples to be used for training the machine. This is an extremely crucial step and the engineer needs to be very careful in deciding the kind of data he wants to use as examples. For instance, for a speech recognition system, the engineer could either use single words, small sentences or entire paragraphs for training the machine.

2. Once the engineer has decided on the type of data he wants to use, he needs to collect data in order to form a training set. This set needs to be representative of all the possibilities of that function. So, the second step requires the engineer to collect inputs and desired outputs for the training process.

3. Now, the next step is to determine how to represent the input data to the machine. This is very important since the accuracy of the machine depends on the input representation of the function. Normally, the representation is done in the form of a vector. This vector generally contains information about various characteristic features of the input. However, the vector should not include information on too many features since this would increase the time taken for training. A larger number of features might also lead to mistakes made by the machine in prediction. The

vector needs to contain exactly enough data to predict outputs.

4. After deciding on the representation of input data, a decision must be made on the structure of the function. The learning algorithm to be used must also be decided on. Most commonly used algorithms are decision trees or support vector machines.

5. Now the engineer must complete the design. The learning algorithm chosen should be run on the data set that has been gathered for training. Sometimes, certain algorithms require the engineer to decide on some control parameters in order to ensure that the algorithm works well. These parameters can be estimated by testing on a smaller subset or by using the method of cross validation.

6. After running the algorithm and generating the function, the accuracy of the function should be calculated. For this, engineers generally use a testing

set. This set of data is different from the training data and the corresponding outputs to the inputs are already known. The test set inputs are sent into the machine and the outputs obtained are checked with those in the test set.

There are a number of supervised learning algorithms in use and each one has its own strengths and weaknesses. Since there is no definitive algorithm that can be used for all instances, the selection of the learning algorithm is a major step in the procedure.

Issues to consider in Supervised Learning: With the usage of supervised learning algorithms, there arise a few issues associated with it. Given below are 4 major issues:

Bias-variance tradeoff
The first issue that needs to be kept in mind while working with machine learning is the bias-variance tradeoff. Consider a situation where we have various different but equally good training sets. If, when a machine is

trained with different data sets, it gives systematically incorrect output predictions for a certain output, the learning algorithm is said to be biased towards that input. A learning algorithm can also be considered to have a high variance for an input. This occurs when the algorithm causes the machine to predict different outputs for that input in each training set. The sum of the bias and variance of the learning algorithm is known as the prediction error for the classifier function. There exists an exchange between variance and bias. A requirement for learning algorithms with low bias is that they need to be flexible enough in order to accommodate all the data sets. However, if they are too flexible, the learning algorithms might end up giving varying outputs for each training set and hence increases the variance. This kind of learning methods needs to be able to amend according to this tradeoff. This is generally done spontaneously or by using an adjustable parameter.

The second issue is concerned with deciding on the amount of training data based on the complexity of the classifier or regression function to be generated. Suppose the function to be generated is simple, a learning algorithm that is relatively inflexible with low variance and high bias will be able to learn from a small amount of training data. However, on many occasions, the function will be complex. This can be the case due to a large number of input features being involved or due to the machine being expected to behave differently for different parts of the input vector. In such cases, the function can only be learned from a large amount of training data. These cases also require the algorithms used to be flexible with low bias and high variance. Therefore, efficient learning algorithms automatically arrive at a tradeoff for the bias and variance depending on the complexity of the function and the amount of training data required.

Yet another issue that needs to be dealt with is the dimensionality of the input vector space. If the input vector includes a large number of features, the learning problem will become difficult even if the function only considers a few of these features as valuable inputs. This is simply because the extra and unnecessary dimensions could lead to confusion and could cause the learning algorithm to have high variance. So, when the input dimensions are large, the classifier is generally adjusted to offset the effects by having low variance and high bias. In practice, the engineer could manually remove the irrelevant features in order to improve the accuracy and efficiency of the learning algorithm. However, this might not always be a practical solution. In recent times, many algorithms have been developed which are capable of removing unnecessary features and retaining only the relevant ones. This concept is known as dimensionality reduction, which helps in mapping input data into lower dimensions in order to improve the performance of the learning algorithm.

Noise in the output values

The final issue on this list is concerned with the interference of noise in the desired output values. It is possible that the values of the desired outputs (supervisory targets) can be wrong due to the noise that gets added at sensors. These values could also be wrong due to human error. In such cases, the learning algorithm should not look to match the training inputs with their exact outputs. For such cases, algorithms with high bias and low variance are desirable.

Other factors to consider

- One important thing to be kept in mind is the heterogeneity of data. The level of heterogeneity of the data should also play a role in dictating the learning algorithm that is to be chosen. Some algorithms work better on data sets whose inputs are limited within small ranges. A few of these are support vector machines, logistic regression, neural networks, linear regression and nearest neighbor methods. Nearest neighbor methods and support vector machines with Gaussian kernels work especially better with inputs limited to small ranges. On the other hand, there exist algorithms like decision trees, which work very well with heterogeneous data sets.

- Another feature of the data sets that needs to be considered is the amount of redundancy in the set. A few algorithms perform poorly in the presence of excessive redundancy. This happens due to numerical instabilities. Examples of these types of algorithms are logistic regression, linear regression, and distance based methods. For such cases, regularization needs to be included so that the algorithms can perform better.

- While choosing algorithms, engineers need to consider the amount of non-linearities in the inputs and the interactions within different features of the input vector. If there is little to no interaction and each feature contributes independently to the output, algorithms based on distance functions and linear functions perform very efficiently. However, when there are a number of interactions within the input features, algorithms based on decision trees and neural networks are desirable. The reason for this is that these algorithms are designed to detect these interactions in the input vectors. If the engineer decides to use linear algorithms, he must specify the interactions that exist.

When an engineer is tasked with selecting an algorithm for a specific application, he may choose to compare various algorithms experimentally in order to decide which one is best suited for the application. However, a large amount of time needs to be invested by the engineer in collecting training data and tuning the algorithm. If provided with a large number of resources, it is advisable to spend more time collecting data than spending time on tuning the algorithm because the latter is extremely tedious. The most commonly used learning algorithms are neural networks, nearest neighbor algorithms, linear and logistic regressions, support vector machines and decision trees.

Chapter 5: Unsupervised Machine Learning

At this point, the reader should be familiar with the concept of supervised machine learning wherein the machine is trained using sets of inputs and outputs that are desired. However, there are other techniques of machine learning. One of these is known as reinforcement learning. In this technique, the machine is designed to interact with its ambient environment through actions. Based on the environment's response to these actions, the machine receives rewards if the environment reacts positively or punishments if it reacts negatively. The machine learns from these reactions and is taught to perform in a manner such that it can maximize the rewards it will obtain in the future. The objective could also be to minimize future punishments. This technique of learning is related to the subjects of control theory in engineering and decision theory in statistics and management sciences.

The main problems studied in these two subjects are more or less equivalent and the solutions are similar as well. However, the two subjects focus on different parts of the problem. There exists another technique of machine learning that is closely related to game theory and also uses reinforcement learning. The idea here is similar to that in reinforcement learning. The machine produces some actions that affect the surrounding environment and it receives rewards or punishments depending on the reaction of the environment. However, the main difference is that the environment is not static. It is dynamic and can include other machines as well. These other machines are also capable of producing actions and receiving rewards (or punishments). So, the objective of the machine is to maximize its future rewards (or minimize its future punishments) taking into account the effects of the other machines in the surroundings.

The application of game theory to such a situation with multiple, dynamic systems is a popular area of research. Finally, the fourth technique is called unsupervised machine learning. In this technique, the machine receives training inputs but it does not receive any target outputs or rewards and punishments for its actions. This begs the question- how can the machine possibly learn anything without receiving any feedback from the environment or having information about target outputs? However, the idea is to develop a structure in the machine to build representations of the input vectors in such a manner that they can be used for other applications such as prediction and decision-making. Essentially, unsupervised learning can be looked at as the machine identifying patterns in input data that would normally go unnoticed. Two of the most popular examples of unsupervised learning are dimensionality reduction and clustering. The technique of unsupervised learning is closely related to the fields of information theory and statistics.

Artificial Intelligence and Data Science

Chapter 6: Artificial Intelligence 101

An amazing development has taken place over the last few years. You may have watched how robots in Star Wars were able to perform so many actions and maybe, just maybe, you would have wondered how wonderful it would have been if this were to happen in this decade. You may not have seen it coming, but this was an inevitable turn of events – the emergence of Artificial Intelligence (AI). Everywhere we look today, we come across a number of intelligent systems that talk to us – Siri, Google Assistant – offering us advice and also offering us recommendations. These systems improve almost every year to improve its interpretation of images, voice recognitions and also to drive cars based on different techniques used by

Facebook and Google's Deep Learning Efforts. Other work always aims to understand and generate machines that would understand our language and communicate with us.

The reemergence of AI has caused a lot of confusion since there are so many companies that have begun to explore the scene. How do we make sense of any of it?

Let us start with a simple definition of AI. Artificial Intelligence or AI is a field of computer science that is aimed at developing computers that are capable of performing tasks that can be done by people, especially those tasks that are considered to be performed by intelligent people.

AI has had a number of excellent runs. In the early sixties, there were great promises that were made about what a machine could do. In the eighties, it was said to revolutionize the way businesses were run. But in those eras, the promises that were made were too difficult to deliver. So what makes the latest developments in AI any different? What makes the systems developed now any different from the diagnostic programs and neural nets of the past? There are a number of reasons why the developments in this era are different from the last.

Increased Computational Resources

The computers we have in this era are faster and can think harder thereby increasing the computational power. The techniques used earlier worked well only in the past, but now there would be a necessity to improve the computational grid and also expand it.

Growth of Data

Over the years, the data collected has increased by a vast amount and this data is being made available to the machines. This increase in the data has given machines much more to think about. This goes to say that learning systems get better at understanding more data and would now be able to look at thousand examples as opposed to only a few hundred.

Deeper Focus

AI has shifted away from looking at smaller aspects of data to look at specific problems. The systems now are capable of thinking about a particular problem as opposed to daydreaming without any problem. Systems like Cortana and Siri work well within limited domains that can be focused and modeled on pulling specific words that you would have said instead of understanding the entire sentence spoken by you.

Knowledge Engineering

The problem and issues with knowledge engineering have been transformed into different aspects of learning. The systems developed these days use their own ways to learn. The bottleneck in the systems in the past helped us add more rules to avoid such bottlenecks in the further processing of data. Most approaches in the modern times focus on learning these rules automatically.

Alternative Reasoning Models

Alternative reasoning models have been adopted which are based on the assumption that the systems do not have to reason like human beings in order to be smart. The machine is allowed to think like a machine.

It is these factors put together that have given the world the first renaissance of intelligent machines that have become a part of our lives and have been adopted in different tools and in workplaces.

Exploring AI

The goal for some developers and researchers is to build a system that has the ability to act and think intelligently the way human beings do. Most others do not care if the system does think like human beings – they are only worried about whether or not the system would do the right thing. Apart from these two schools of thought, there are others that are somewhere in between. If we were to use human reasoning in systems, it would help computers do things similar to human beings.

Strong AI

The work that is aimed at stimulating human reasoning in a machine is what is called strong AI. This implies that any machine created would need to have the capabilities of obtaining the results and also explain how a human being would think. Genuine models of AI systems that are simulations of the human mind and cognition have to be built.

Weak AI

The work that was done within the second school of thought, aimed towards just getting structures to work, is commonly known as weak AI in that even as we might be able to build structures which can behave like people, the outcomes tell us nothing about how human beings think or feel. One of the best examples of this is IBM's Deep Blue, a gadget that became a master chess player but absolutely did not play in the same manner that human beings do and informed us very little about cognition in general.

Anything in Between

The systems in between Weak and Strong AI are those that are informed and understand human reasoning but are not slaves to it. This is where most of the powerful work is happening in AI today. This work uses human emotion and reasoning as a guide but it does not use it as a goal to model the system. If only one were able to come up with a name for this school of thought – maybe Practical AI.

The important takeaway is that a system does not have to be smart the way human beings are smart in order for it to be AI. The system would just need to be smart.

Chapter 7: Big Data and Artificial Intelligence

Most AI Systems have started to use three components of human reasoning – assessing, inferring and predicting. There are a number of questions that would need to be answered every day – what is happening around us, what it means, what will happen next and so on. When we push the call button, walk towards and elevator or wait for a taxi, we are trying to assess, infer and predict. AI systems have started to do the same thing, although they would not wait in line to catch a taxi.

In the world of Big Data, where at least 2.5 quintillion bytes of data are collected or produced every single day, it important to know how AI Systems would capture that data, synthesize it and use it to drive their reasoning. The use of AI systems in issues like Big Data allows us to transform the world of numbers and unstructured data into knowledge that can be used by human beings.

The trick to understanding these systems is to understand that the processes that underlie the intelligence that are smart. The systems are built on a foundation that processes are not only simple but also understandable. It is important to remember that AI is not magic but it is the application of algorithms that are powered by data, processing power and scale.

What is Big Data?

Data that is obtained from two significantly different sources is grouped under the banner of Big Data. The first source of data is the data that is found within the organization or business and that is shared across a vast network. This data includes PDF documents, blogs, emails, work documents, business events, internal files, process events and any other structured data, unstructured or semi – structured data that can be found within the organization. The second source of data would be the data that is available outside the organization. Most of this information is available for free but there is some information that would require a certain payment to be made in order to obtain it. Most of this information is available to the general public, but there is some information that is considered confidential and is kept within the organization itself. This information includes literature on products that is distributed by the competitors, information available on social media, hints from third parties, certain organization hierarchies and also any complaints that may have been posted by customers on regulatory sites.

You may begin to wonder what makes Big Data any different from the data that is being used since the ancient times. There are four characteristics of Big Data that make is very different from other kinds of data – Volume, Velocity, Variety, and Veracity. There are a number of other characteristics that differentiate Big Data from other types of data, but these are the most important and prominent characteristics to consider.

Volume

Numerous organizations have started to struggle with the amount of data that is being stored in their data warehouses since big data took the world by a storm. It was noted in the Fortune magazine that the world had already created close to 10 exabytes of data by the year 2006 and that this number would double by the year 2015. It has also been identified that this amount of data can now be collected within a few nanoseconds thereby increasing the data collected by trillion gigabytes every hour, which is a scary amount of data.

A few years ago, there were organizations that would count their data storage space for any type of analytics in terabytes. Now, they can only do the same in petabytes since the data collected has doubled or tripled since then. The amount of data does cause a strain on the analytics architecture for different organizations in different industries. For instance, let us consider an organization that is in the communication industry. You know that this organization would definitely have a hundred million customers. If data were collected for these customers on a daily basis, there would be at least 5 petabytes of data in a hundred days. Most companies try to get rid of data daily, but regulators have asked most companies in the communication industry to store records about calls made or the data used by each customer.

Velocity can be understood from two different perspectives – one that represents latency while the other represents the throughput of data. Let us first take a look at latency. The analytics infrastructure was once a store – and – report environment where the data that was collected the previous day was used to make reports and this data was represented as "D-1." Over the last decade, the analytics infrastructure has been used in different business processes that there was a necessity to change the infrastructure to cater to the needs of all businesses. For example, some advertising agencies are trying to conduct analytics to help them place advertisements on online platforms within 10 milliseconds.

Let us now consider the second measure of velocity – the throughput of data. This represents the data that is flowing through the pipes of the analytics infrastructure. The amount of global mobile data is growing at the rate of 80 percent, which is said to compound annually implying that the data that is collected annually is set to increase by 12 – 14 exabytes per year as users begin to share more images and videos with the world. In order to analyze this data, many corporates are seeking analytical infrastructure that will help them process information in parallel.

Variety

It was in the late 1990s that Data Warehouse Technology was introduced to create and represent data using Meta – models that would help to simplify data and also help to represent data collected in one form, irrespective of whether or not the data was structured.

The data was often compiled from multiple sources and was then transformed using either ETL (Extract, Transform, Load) or ELT (Extract data, load it into the warehouse and transform the data within the warehouse). The idea was to narrow down the variety and ambiguity in the data collected and also structure that data to put it to good use. Big Data has helped to expand our horizons by enabling new data integration and solutions infrastructure and data analytics technology. A number of call center analytics constantly seek solutions that would help them attend to their customers better. These solutions would also help them understand the conversation that takes place between them and the disgruntled customer, which would then give them an idea of how to proceed further. The source data that is obtained from call centers are only unstructured data like audio, sound, or text and some structured data. Different applications gather different types of data from blogs, emails, and documents. For example, Slice, a company used to provide analytics for online orders, uses raw data that comes from a number of different organizations like online bookstore purchases, airline tickets, parking tickets, music download receipts and any other purchases that may have hit your email. How can this information be normalized into creating product catalogs and also analyze any purchases made?

Veracity

Internal data is often carefully governed while Big Data comes from a number of sources that are outside the control of the company and this data often comes with a lot of inaccuracies and incorrectness, which would hamper the analysis made. Veracity represents the sustainability of the data obtained and also looks for the credibility of the sources of data that is obtained for a target audience.

Let us try to see how we can understand the credibility of the sources of data. If organizations began to collect information on their own products using third parties and then provide that information to their customer care support or their contact center employees in order to support the queries that customers have, the organizations providing the information would need to be assessed and screened before trusting the information that is provided by them. Otherwise, there can be a possibility of the organization making a wrong offer to the customer thereby affecting the revenue. Numerous social media responses to different campaigns could come from unhappy customers or disgruntled employees, which would definitely impact the decisions made by the company. For instance, if there was a survey conducted by companies on the products provided by them and customers happened to like the product, this would be taken into consideration. However, if the customer were to select an option that did not show that they liked the product, it is important to know why before taking this unstructured piece of data into account.

We have to always consider the amount of truth that can be shared with an audience. The veracity of the data that is collected or created within a given organization is often considered to be well intentioned. However, some of that data cannot be shared with the public since there could be some threat to the company. This would reduce the chance of having a wider communication network. For instance, if customer service has provided the manufacturing and engineering department with the shortcomings of a particular product based on the feedback given by customers, the data shared should be selective and on a need – to – know basis only. Other data can be shared with some customers who have certain prerequisites or contracts.

Big Data makes it possible for numerous businesses to process all the information that is collected on the simple learning systems. They would need to identify one signal from all the noise. It is only through this way of learning that it is possible to translate sentences from one language to the other. Parallelism and processing enable systems to take up thousands of pieces of evidence and then test them independently before adding up the results.

Assessing Data using AI

Consumer systems always try to assess human beings. For examples, Amazon puts together a picture of who you are and what products interest you and also assesses you against other similar customers and makes predictions about you. The data that is used to make this prediction is transactional – what you look at and what you purchase. Amazon's recommendation engines use all this information to come to a conclusion of what products should be recommended to you.

Profile data is only a small part of the picture. To this data, information about different categories – cluster objects (DIY books), Customers and other information – would need to be assessed to make an informed decision. The area you live in and the amount of money you would be willing to spend can be pulled in to refine the assumptions made about you.

The results are always a set of characterizations:

- Based on what collections you like, you have a lot in common with a person across the globe that has a similar interest in science fiction, DIY books, and cookbooks and so on.

- Based on a set of things you were looking at, you could be someone who loves to garden.
- You just bought gardening tools to create your own kitchen garden.

For retailers, the information that is of utmost importance is transactions, product categories and the clusters of people. For search engines, the important information is the history of the information you have looked for and also the items you have clicked on and at which location those clicks were made.

Chapter 8: How does AI draw conclusions from Data?

There are different methods that can be used by learning systems to infer something from data. This chapter covers the most common methods used for the same.

Deductive Reasoning

Deductive reasoning ensures that the system comes up with a distinct solution. The process starts with the assertion of a rule or assumption and then proceeds from there to arrive at the conclusion. The assumption made in this form of reasoning is that if the original rule or assumption made is true, then the conclusion is definitely true. For instance,

If x = 3

And y = 4

Then, 4x+2y = 20

In the above example, there exists a logical necessity that $(4x+2y)$ is equal to 20. The symbolic logic in the above equations uses a language that helps the system come to this conclusion. But, if there were no equations and only English sentences were being used, there would be no difficulty to come to a conclusion if the system were to use deductive syllogism. For instance,

The disorder in a system would increase unless energy is used. If my bedroom were a system, then disorder would constantly increase unless I was to clean the room.

In the syllogism given above, the first statement and the second statement lead to the conclusion that the room would need to be cleaned to avoid having any disorder in it. Consider another example:

Medical technology, if used successfully to treat patients, should be funded. Stem cells have been used to treat patients successfully using sixty new therapies. Stem cell research and technology should be funded.

A conclusion that is made is considered true or false depending on the premise of the argument. However, the deductive inference can be considered true or false irrespective of whether or not the premise is true. The final conclusion can be valid even if the premise is false. For instance,

Drought does not exist in the West.

Las Vegas is in the West.

People living in Las Vegas do not have to worry about dealing with drought.

The inferential process is valid and the conclusion obtained based on the premises is also valid. However, this conclusion is unsound since the premise itself is unsound. This form of a syllogism is very deceiving since it looks very logical and to be very fair, it is logical. But, if the premise were incorrect, the conclusion obtained would never serve the purpose of the exercise.

If the assumption were made that propositions are sound, the stern logic and process followed in deductive reasoning would give conclusions that are absolutely certain. Deductive reasoning cannot enhance the workings of an AI system because the conclusions are often self – evident. The system would be unable to make a prediction about the future.

Inductive Reasoning

Inductive reasoning starts with making observations that are limited to the scope of the issue and ends with making a generalized conclusion, one that is likely but is not certain since the conclusion is based on accumulated evidence. Inductive reasoning moves from specific conclusions to general conclusions. AI systems often use inductive reasoning to obtain conclusions. They gather evidence, seek patterns and form hypotheses or theories to explain what has occurred.

Conclusions that are obtained using inductive methods of reasoning need not be logical. No amount of evidence obtained would guarantee the conclusion. This is for the reason that there is absolutely no way to confirm that all the evidence necessary to derive the conclusion has been drawn and that there is no other unobserved evidence that exists to validate that hypothesis. Newspapers could report a number of conclusions that could have been obtained by AI but there is an important aspect to consider – AI can only envision what could possibly happen, it cannot be certain of the outcome of events when using inductive reasoning.

Since inductive conclusions need not be logical, the arguments are most often not true. They are cogent, implying that the evidence seems relevant, complete and convincing to an extent that the conclusion could be true. It can also be said that inductive arguments are not false; the right term would be that they are not cogent.

This is an important difference between inductive and deductive reasoning. While inductive reasoning cannot yield absolute conclusions, it can increase the knowledge that the AI system has. It can help the system make predictions about the future.

For instance, Albert Einstein had observed the way a pocket compass moved when he was five years old. He then became fascinated by the idea of something invisible causing the compass needle to move. This observation followed by a number of other observations and the use of mathematical and logical tools helped him derive a conclusion that helped him predict events that were yet to be observed. AI learning system using inductive reasoning can perform the same actions.

Abductive Reasoning

This type of reasoning begins with a set of observations that are incomplete and then proceeds to form the most likely explanation for that very set of observations. Abductive reasoning helps to derive conclusions that would help to make the right decisions on a daily basis using the information that is at hand, which is often incomplete.

For instance, a doctor would give his diagnosis based on abductive reasoning. He would take a look at the symptoms and try to identify the diagnosis that would explain those very symptoms. The same goes for when jurors listen to a criminal case. The jurors would need to consider the evidence produced by both the defense and the prosecution and make an informed decision covering all points of the evidence collected. There could be no certainty about the verdict since most evidence would not have been admitted to them during the case, but they would make their best guess. The same goes for AI learning systems. They would make informed decisions and come to the right conclusions using whatever information they are provided with.

Inductive reasoning works on the principle that the evidence obtained does not necessarily have to be complete to make a decision. However, when it comes to abductive reasoning, it is important that the evidence obtained is complete in order to make informed decisions or even predict the future. For instance, a doctor may look at only a certain number of symptoms to make his prognosis, but he would be making the best use of those symptoms.

The process of abductive reasoning is creative, intuitive and can also be revolutionary. For instance, Einstein's work was not only deductive and inductive; it also involved a lot of creativity and imagination, which was scarcely warranted at that time. Einstein only made thought-based judgments and it was for this reason that most of his peers did not trust his theories. His theories have proved to be correct to this day!

Case Based Reasoning

The earlier methods use different premises and assumptions to identify and represent the data collected and then use that data to predict the future. However, in case based reasoning, the premises and assumptions are stored and are accessed to solve future problems. If the system were looking at a new problem, it would look for premises and assumptions that were similar to the new problem and use those cases to predict the target future value. This is one of the easier ways of obtaining a conclusion using an AI system since there is relatively less work that will need to be done offline. The cases used are already stored in the warehouse that can be used by the system.

Regression and classification use case based reasoning. This reasoning is also applicable when the premises and cases are complicated, such as in criminal cases where the cases are often complicated laws and legal rulings and also in planning where the cases are prior solutions to complex problems.

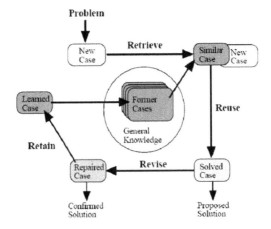

If the cases and premises are simple, only one algorithm can be run to use the case or premise that is similar to the new problem at hand. The system would then create a set of these similar cases and use those as input to predict the target future value.

Common Sense Reasoning

The ability of human beings to use common sense knowledge is completely dependent on their ability to perform common sense reasoning.

Most artificial intelligence systems have not been designed to infer using the rules of any of the well-known concepts of mathematical logic. There is no distinction between the inferences that are correct and the inferences that would need to be used to solve the problem at hand. However, the logical system often corresponds to the subset of first order logic. Systems often provide for the path to infer a fact about a particular object using other facts and objects that contain variables with general rules. However, many systems never infer statements that are general – they never look for quantified formulae.

Human reasoning involves the process of obtaining facts by making observations in the world and now, computer programs are also capable of doing the same. Robert Filman conducted an interesting thesis on observation in the chess world where he concluded that people obtained many facts using observation although they could use deduction to obtain those very same results. Some smart systems would not need to have the skill to observe, but if we were to build a system that would try to diagnose and draw conclusions from the patient's appearance, it is important to build systems with better observation skills.

An important development in AI is the use of non-monotonic reasoning to make the right judgments and conclusions.

Deductive reasoning is based on mathematical logic and has the property of monotonicity where the system would obtain an analogy using similar mathematical concepts. Let us assume we have a set of premises or assumptions to solve one problem. Now, we add additional premises and assumptions to the set. There could be new conclusions obtained but every sentence that was obtained after a thorough deduction would still be connected to the enlarged set.

Human reasoning does not ordinarily share the monotonicity property. If you knew that I owned a car, you would ask me to give you a ride when you needed one. If you knew that my car was being serviced, which does not change the fact that you knew that I owned a car, you would not ask me for a ride. If I told you that my car would be out in half an hour, you will probably change your mind and ask me again.

A number of artificial intelligence researchers have pointed out that computer programs that are intelligent would need to reason non-monotonically. Based on this observation, some concluded that logic could not be used always.

However, it was seen that deductive reasoning could be substituted with additional modes of non-monotonic reasoning, which are as accurate and precise as deduction and can be studied mathematically. Non-monotonic reasoning has become more formalized and gives rules of conjecture. However these rules of inference imply that the conclusions drawn could be appropriate but could be proved wrong if more facts are obtained.

Chapter 9: What is Data Science?

Data science is one of the emerging fields in statistics that analogous to the collection, preparation, analysis, visualization, management and preparation of vast amount of information or data. The term is connected to and refers to a number of areas of study including computer science and databases, but there are a set of skills that one would need to possess, including non – mathematical skills, to work as a successful data scientist.

For some, the term data science conjures an image of a statistician in a white lab coat staring at the computer screen and scrolling through numbers. This is far from the truth. Statisticians do not wear coats – you may find them in thick glasses – but this statement of fashion is reserved only for environmentalists, doctors, biologists and scientists who work in environments that are not clothes friendly. Also, the data that is collected is never structured. This implies that the data that is received could be of different kinds – audio, video or even text. Think about a website that is filled with pictures and messages from friends or other users – there is absolutely no way you can find numbers on that page.

It is a known fact that most schools, governments, and companies use enormous amounts of information in the form of numbers – grades, tax, revenues – but there is enormous data that is collected by these organizations that are not structured. The latter form of information makes most statisticians and mathematicians cringe. It is always useful to have people with great mathematical skills, but there is a lot more to data than just math. It is essential to know if people working on data are comfortable with trying to analyze images, words, paragraphs, sounds, videos, lists and various other forms of information.

In addition to the different kinds of data, data science is a lot more than just the analysis and management of information or data collected. There are a number of people who would love to analyze the data collected and spend hours or years looking at plots or histograms, but for those people who prefer to look at more than just plots data science offers a number of roles that would cater to different skill sets. Let us take a look at the different types of data that would need to be considered when it comes to buying a floor cleaning detergent.

Irrespective of what your preference is to buy a detergent – fresh smelling, colorful, good reviews – you prepare yourself to buy this particular commodity when you write it down on your grocery list. You would consider this list to be a small scribble that you will throw out when you finish shopping. When you enter the store, you would remember to buy floor-cleaning detergent because of the list in your hands. At the checkout, the cashier would scan the barcode of the product and the register would log the price. In the data warehouse, the computer would make note that there is one less item available for the same product. This will give the stock manager an idea of how much of the product he would need to buy in the future. If you have a coupon on the product, you would get a discount and the computer will also note this. At the end of the week, the information with respect to the detergent would be uploaded and sent to the detergent company. The company would then pay the discounted amount to the grocery store. At the end of the month, the manager of the store would then create graphs and pie charts, which would show the different detergents sold at the store and how many orders should be placed for the different kinds of detergent.

This tiny piece of data that was on a small sheet of paper has now ended up on different servers in different warehouses. This piece of information would have ended up on the manager's desk and he would need to make a decision on whether or not he would need to place an order for the detergent. This piece of information went from the tiny piece of paper on to the manager's desk. This information would not have been sent in its raw form to the manager's desk – it would have been transformed. In addition to the different computers used and the software used on those computers, other hardware like the barcode scanner comes into picture. All of these put together will help to scan, collect, manipulate, transmit and store the data, which would then be analyzed by the manager.

Data scientists definitely do not take part in each step of the process. They are not a part of the process where hardware would be built to collect the necessary information. You may be wondering where they would be coming into picture. Data scientists play the most active role in these aspects called the four A's of data: Data Architecture, Data Acquisition, Data Analysis and Data Archiving. Let us take a look at the detergent example. With respect to the data architecture, it is important that in the design of the system for sale to think in advance about how the data coming out of the system would be used. The system architect would have a keen appreciation that both the stock and store manager would need to use the data that is scanned at the cash register, for similar purposes. A data scientist would help the architect by providing input on how the data would be used and how it would need to be routed and organized to support the visualization, analysis and presentation of the data to the right people.

Next acquisition focuses on how the data are to be collected and how they would need to be represented before the analysis of the data begins. For instance, every barcode represents a number that does not describe the product itself. At what point must the barcode be associated with the description of the product that it was printed on? Different barcodes are used for the exact same product. When should we make note of the fact that both Products X and Y are the same but have different barcodes? Representation, transforming, grouping and linking of data are all tasks that will need to be performed before the data can be analyzed for profitability. These are the tasks where the data scientist is involved.

The analysis phase is where the data scientist is most involved. In this context, we would be using analysis to summarize the data that was collected, using certain segments of the data to make inferences about the data as a whole. This analysis would then be presented in tables, graphs, charts, and animations. There are many technical, statistical and mathematical aspects to these activities but it is important to remember that the ultimate audience for data analysis is in fact a person or a group of people. These people are the data users and it is these people's needs that data scientists would be fulfilling. This point highlights the need for excellent communication skills in data science. The most sophisticated statistical analysis developed would not be worth anything unless the results that have been created can be communicated effectively to the data user.

Data scientists would need to become actively involved in the process of archiving the data collected and analyzed. The data or information would need to be preserved in a manner that would make the data useful in the future. This could be termed as data curation and the process is a difficult challenge since it is always difficult to anticipate the use of that data in the future. For instance, when developers of twitter were working on how to store tweets, they never anticipated that these tweets could be used to pinpoint earthquakes and tsunamis, but they had enough foresight to realize that these "geocodes" could be useful elements to store as data.

Python

Chapter 10: Markov's Model in Python

Now that we have taken a look at Markov Models, Hidden Markov Models, Machine Learning, Artificial Intelligence and Data Science, let us take a look at how to apply our knowledge of the Markov Models in Python.

Python is a simple but powerful language that was developed in the 1980s by Guido van Rossum. This language is a favorite for those who love to code for the purpose of machine learning. Let us first take a look at how to start working in Python before we look at programming Markov Models.

Getting Started

There are different ways to start working in Python depending on the type of OS you use – Windows, Linus or Mac OSX. This section takes you through the steps you would need to follow for the different systems.

Linux

Step 1: Connect to the Internet.

Step 2: Launch the Terminal Application.

Step 3: Type "su" in the command prompt window and press enter.

Step 4: Type the root password and press enter.

Step 5: There are different ways to install Python on the two types of Linus -

Debian Based – Type "apt-get install Python" and press enter.

Redhat/RHEL/Cent OS – Type, "yum install Python" and press enter.

Step 6: Once the installation process is complete, update the system by typing "su-apt get update" and press enter.

Step 1: Go to the website: https://www.python.org/downloads/windows to download Python.

Step 2: Choose the bits based on your Windows software.

Step 3: Open the Python.exe file.

Step 4: Click "Accept Default Settings".

Step 5: Wait for the installation process to complete.

Python 2.7 is already installed on Mac OSX, but if you would like to use the latest version, follow the steps below.

Step 1: Open any of the OSX emulators.

Step 2: Type "/user/bin/ruby_e"$(curl_fsSL http://raw.githubusercontent.com/homebrew/install/master/install)"

Step 3: Wait for the installation process to complete.

Step 4: Go to "~/.profile" ad, "export PATH=/user/local/bin:/usr/local/sbin: $PATH"

Step 5: Install Python language interpreter by typing "Brew install Python".

Step 6: Wait for the installation process to complete.

Once you have installed Python, you can use your coding application to work on programming Markov Models using Python.

Programming a Hidden Markov Model

Let us take a look at the different components we will be using.

Import numpy as np

Import pandas as pd

Import netwrokx as nx

Import matplotlib.pyplot as plt

%matplotlib inline

Next, we will need to input all the information we have on the Markovian model being considered.

The variables that we need to know are the states, the probabilities of transition from one state to the other (A) and the emission probabilities (B), the initial probability distribution P an any other information that can be found. Let us take the example of a baby. There would be three states that the baby would normally be in "sleep", "eat" and "cry". This can be represented as follows:

S = {sleep, eat, cry}

We would then need to look at the probabilities of the states and also look at the initial probability distribution P. Let us assume that there is a 40% chance of the baby sleeping, 35% chance of the baby crying and 25% chance of the baby eating. This would mean:

P = {0.40, 0.35, 0.25}

This information is represented as follows in Python:

States = ['sleeping', 'eating', ' crying']

P= [0.40, 0.25, 0.35]

State_space = pd.Series(pi, index = states, name = 'states')

Print(state_space) #ensure that the states and their probabilities are matched correctly

Print(state_space.sum()) #ensure that the probabilities add up to 1

You have to identify some output that would match each state correctly and also provide you with a distribution where the probability sum up to 1. You have to ensure that you do not use any symbolic notations in Python since the language would not accept those.

Let us now input the state transition probabilities. Let us assume that the probabilities are as follows:

Sleeping -> Sleeping = 0.40

Sleeping -> Eating = 0.20

Sleeping -> Crying = 0.40

Eating -> Sleeping = 0.45

Eating -> Eating = 0.45

Eating -> Crying = 0.10

Crying -> Sleeping = 0.45

Crying -> Eating = 0.25

Crying -> Crying = 0.30

Note: '->' indicates moving from one state to the other.

This information would need to be inputted into Python in the following manner:

O_df = pd.DataFrame (columns = states, index = states)

O_df.loc [states[0]] = [0.4, 0.2, 0.4]

O_df.loc [states[1]] = [0.45, 0.45, 0.1]

O_df.loc [states[2]] = [0.45, 0.25, 0.3]

Print (O_df)

O=O_df.values #ensure that the matrix has been created correctly and the values are all placed correctly

Print ('\n',O,O.shape,'\n\) #ensure that the shape of the matrix is right

Print (O_df.sum(axis=1)) #ensure that the probabilities add up to 1

Printing this will show the matrix to you and will give you the exact shape of the matrix (3x3). The sum of the individual probabilities will help you identify if the total is 1 or lesser than 1. Make sure that you change the probabilities appropriately if there is any discrepancy.

In order to make this a Hidden Markov Model, you would need to recognize certain factors of the baby which would make him move into one of the states mentioned. For instance, if the baby were sick, he or she would probably wail throughout the night. If he or she were completely healthy, it would be a whole other state. There will need to be a set of probabilities that would need to be created in order to take these states into account – since it is really likely for the baby to be healthy or sick.

Hidden_states = ['healthy', ' sick'0

P = [0.5,0.5]

State_space=   pd.Series   (P,   index   = hidden_states, name= 'states')

Print (state_space) #make sure that the hidden states and probabilities have been matched correctly

Print ('\n', state_space.sum()) #ensure that the probabilities are equal to 1

We will need to print one more time to ensure that the states and probabilities have been matched perfectly and that the total probability is equal to 1.

We would now need to input the emission probabilities.

Observable_states = states

B_df = pd.DataFrame (columns = observable_states, index = hidden_states)

B_df.loc[hidden_states[0]] = [0.2,0.6,0.2]

B_df.loc[hidden_states[1]] = [0.4,0.1,0.5]

Print(B_df)

B=B_df.values   #ensure that the values correspond to the states

Print ('\n',B,B.shape,'\n') #ensure that the emission probabilities add up to 1

This matrix should be 2x3, which represents the two hidden states and the three observed states.

You have successfully created a Markov Model for a baby. You can use a similar program to create another Markov Model for the weather and verify if you have understood the concepts well.

Conclusion

I want to thank you once again for choosing this book.

You should now have a better understanding of the Markov Model and also learn to program the basic Markov Model on Python.

To summarize, we have looked at the axioms that one would need to be clear with when learning Markov Models. These included a number of axioms that are integral to Markov Models. We then looked at Markov Models and Hidden Markov Models and covered some aspects of Markov Models. We then looked at Data Mining and also tried to understand different aspects of Data Mining. We answered the question of how Data Mining is used and also tried to see why it is used.

We then covered machine learning and looked at Supervised and Unsupervised Machine learning in great detail. We looked at the different ways in which machine learning is used and also its applications. We also took a look at artificial intelligence and how it is important in big data analysis. This chapter also covered certain reasoning skills used by AI Systems to understand data and come to a conclusion or predict the future. We then looked at how Data Science plays a key role in Artificial Intelligence.

The last section of the book deals with creating a Markov Model using Python. It has been explained very clearly in the book how a user can download and use Python. A sample code has been provided to you in the chapter, which will help you fit a three state Markov Model. However, you have to remember that this model is only code and it can be tweaked for your purposes.

By now, you should feel comfortable with the different terms in machine learning and also understand the mathematical aspects that lie behind it. I hope you feel more informed about the coding and mathematics that drives a great deal of data that is collected and used in the data science and artificial intelligence industries. I hope you are inspired to learn more.

If you thought 2 books was an incredible deal, well I got great news for you! I'm all about giving back, especially with all the knowledge and opportunities I have gained over the years. I want to give you as much value as possible within this bundle book.

Turn the page for a BONUS BOOK, COMPLETELY FREE!

Enjoy :D

Sincerely,

W. Svillan

William Sullivan

DATA

ANALYTICS GUIDE
FOR BEGINNERS

INTRODUCTION

William Sullivan

Data Analytics Guide: For Beginners Introduction

Table of Contents

advice. Please consult a licensed professional before attempting any techniques outlined in this book.

By reading this document, the reader agrees that under no circumstances are is the author responsible for any losses, direct or indirect, which are incurred as a result of the use of information contained within this document, including, but not limited to, —errors, omissions, or inaccuracies

Introduction

Congratulations on purchasing/downloading this book !

The following chapters we'll discuss are going to inform you of everything that you need to know in order to analyze data. Whenever you are analyzing data, you are going to be taking data and modifying it, inspecting it, creating models of the data, and even cleaning up the data so that it can be used in the equations that you need to use it in.

Data analytics is used in the real world in a lot of jobs that you may be looking to get yourself into. In order to get yourself into data analytics and get hired into a job that will pay you more money, you are going to want to ensure that you have everything that you need to know under your belt so that you are placing yourself one step ahead of the competition and get yourself hired!

When you are doing data analysis, you are going to be taking raw data that you gathered from your sources and turning it into information that you are going to find more useful not only to you, but to others too. All of the data that you collect is going to come from you answering a question or testing a hypothesis or even when you are trying to disprove a theory.

You are going to have to keep in mind that there are going to be multiple phases that you are going to go through in order to work with the data that you collect so that it can be analyzed correctly. You should not be surprised if one of the phases means that there is going to be extra work on your end in previous steps so that you are getting the appropriate data analysis.

At the point in time that data is placed into an analysis program, you are going to have to go on the parameters that are set into place either by you or the person who is making the decisions to make sure that you are making sure that your consumer is getting an excellent product.

Most of the data that you are going to be analyzing is going to be collected through an innovative process such as going to a particular area in a neighborhood and collecting information from that specific community. From there, the variables are going to be broken down based on the individuals who fit into groups such as age, income, so on and so forth. Your data is going to categorical or numerical depending on what you are trying to figure out.

As you go about collecting your data, you are going to need to follow all of the requirements that are going to keep you on track for the study. In other words, you are not going to want to ask about someone's favorite movie when you are trying to discover how many children they have. There are going to be sensors that you are going to use such as traffic cameras or environmental sensors that are going to give you all of the data that you want to know. Not only that, but you can do an interview face to face in order to obtain the data that you need.

Once you have collected all of the data that you need, then you are going to be at the step where you are going to be ready to share the data that you have analyzed. In the end, the result is going to require that you get feedback from your consumer so that you can help make sure that your company is running more efficiently so that you can ensure that you are getting the product out to the customer that they are wanting. In other words, you are going to be making sure that you are not putting out a defective product that no one is going to buy.

There are going to be times that you are going to have to use visualization tools to make sure that you are sharing the data in a way that everyone understands. Not everyone is going to be able to understand the data by being told a variety of number.

There are plenty of books on this subject on the market, thanks again for choosing this one! Every effort was made to ensure it is full of as much useful information as possible, please enjoy!

Description

Data analytics is used in the real world in a lot of jobs that you may be looking to get yourself into. In order to get yourself into data analytics and get hired into a job that will pay you more money, you are going to want to ensure that you have everything that you need to know under your belt so that you are placing yourself one step ahead of the competition and get yourself hired!

The chapter discussions of this book are going to inform you of everything that you need to know in order to analyze data.

These include :

- Things you need to know about regression analysis and social network analysis
- What are big data, data and text mining, and web scraping and their applications in the real world
- Techniques in data analysis

- Learn how to reduce your workload through data reduction
- Risks that you have to know in order to protect yourself, your company, and your data
- And so much more...

Chapter 1: Regression Analysis

When dealing with statistical models, you are going to use regression analysis. Regression analysis is a process that you are going to be determining what relationships there are amongst all of the variables that are being used. Using techniques such as modeling and analyzing the variables will be included whenever the focus is on the relationship that falls between the independent and the dependent variables.

In other words, regression analysis is going to assist the user in understanding that how the usual value for the dependent variable is going to change whenever one of the independent variables remains unchanged while other independent variables are changed. Estimating the conditional expectation for the dependent variable depending on what the independent variable is one of the most common regression analysis.

The less common use is going to be on quantile or the location parameter for the distribution of the dependent variable given what independent variables are being used. Nonetheless, all cases when regression analysis is used is going to be to target the function of the independent variables.

Regression models

There are three variables that all regression models will have.

Your dependent variable will be y.

The independent variable will be x.

Finally, the unknown parameters are going to be denoted with the beta symbol. Which is going to be represented as the scalar or the vector.

There are going to be a lot of different fields for applications which are going to consist of various terms that are going to be used to describe the independent and dependent variables.

Regression models are going to relate the dependent variable to the function of the independent variable and the unknown parameters.

$$Y \approx f(x, \beta) Y \approx f(x, \beta)$$

In other words, it is going to be formalized as

$$E(Y|X) = f(x, \beta)$$

This is done in order to carry out the regression analysis. In each expression, f has to be specified. There are going to be times that this form is going to be based on the information that you gathered about the connection between x and y while it does not depend on the data that you have obtained. If there is no knowledge available, there is going to be a convenient or flexible form that f is going to be chosen for.

You are going to assume now that the vector for your parameters of beta is going to be the length of k. So, the user is going to have to provide the information for the dependent variable to be able to get a regression analysis.

In the event that the n data points for y and x are observed, then n is going to be less than k in most of the classical approaches that you are going to see in regression analysis and if this happens, then there will be no performed analysis. This happens because the equations' system is going to define the regressions model for the undetermined. There is also not going to be enough data for you to be able to recover beta.

If n is equal to the k data points, then the function of f will end up being linear. Your equation is going to be $y = f\left(X, \beta\right) y = f\left(X, \beta\right)$ which is going to be able to able to be solved exactly rather than give you an approximation. Therefore, you are going to be reducing your work because you are only going to be solving the n set of equations in which n's unknowns are going to be the elements of beta. As long as x is linearly independent, there will always be a unique solution. Therefore, the solution is not going to exist or there are going to be multiple solutions in case f will be nonlinear.

Another common situation you are going to see is when n is greater than the k data points that are being observed. If you find yourself working with this situation then there is going to be enough information in your hands to be able to estimate what the value of beta is going to best fit the data that you are working with. So, your regression model is going to be viewed as an over determined system inside of beta.

When working with the last regression analysis that was mentioned you are going to have the tools provided to you so that you can find a solution for your parameters of beta. Not only that, but under some statistical assumptions, the analysis is going to use the extra data that you have so that you can predict what your dependent variable is.

Independent measurements

When looking at regression models, there are going to be three unknown parameters. If you look at an experiment where there are ten measurements that are all the same value for the independent variable vector X, there is going to be that many independent variables. So, for this example, there are going to be three independent variables.

In this instance, the regression analysis is going to fail to result in a unique set of values that were estimated for the parameters this experiment did not provide you with enough data. Therefore, you can estimate the average value and the standard deviation for your dependent variables.

On the same hand, you are going to be measuring two different values for your independent variable in order to get enough information for the regression of two of your parameters but not for three or more of those that you do not know.

If there had been different measurements with three different values, then you would have received a unique set of estimations for your parameters.

Therefore, you are going to strive to have different numbered measurements so that you can figure out what your beta is going to be.

Underlying assumptions

Some of the more classical assumptions that you are going to see in data analysis are:

1. The samples that are going to be representative of the population of the inference predictions.
2. If there is an error it is going to be the random variable which is going to mean that you have zero conditions on the analytical variables.
3. Without errors, your independent variables are going to be measured. Keep in mind that if this

does not happen, then the modeling can be done rather than using an error in variables model.

4. Independent variables will be linearly independent which means it is not possible to show the predictors as a linear combination.

5. Errors are going to be uncorrelated which means that your variance covariance matrix for your errors is going to be diagonal and every element that is not zero will be a variance of the error that you are seeing.

6. Variance for the errors will be constant across all of your observations. If you find that this is not the case, then you can use the weighted least squares method.

Power and simple sized calculations

When talking about regression analysis, there are not any methods that have been agreed upon when it comes to the number of independent variables against the number of observations that you are going to find inside of a model. One rule that you are going to want to try and follow is $N = m^n$ in which n is going to be the size of the sample, the superscript n is going to be how many independent variables there are in the equation, and m is how many observations that are needed in order to reach the precision that you want.

Take for example that there is a researcher that is trying to build a linear regression model by using the data that they collected from over a thousand different patients in their local hospital. The number of patients is going to be N. but, what happens if the researcher decides to take five of those thousand observations and decides that they need to create a straight line? This is going to be the m in your equation because the maximum number of independent variables that you are going to be able to have is 4.

Log 1000/log 5 = 4.29

Other methods to use with regression analysis

Because the parameters that you find in a regression model are typically going to be an estimation due to the method used. Some of these methods are:

1. The Bayesian method or the Bayesian linear regression
2. Distance metric learning. You are going to learn this by searching for the meaningful distance metric inside of any given input space.
3. Percentage regression. You are going to find that for most situations where you are reducing the percentage errors to find the one that is more appropriate.
4. Nonparametric regression. This method is going to require a lot of observations and is going to be intensive when it comes to the calculations.
5. Least absolute deviations are going to be one of the more robust outlines which are going to end up leading you into doing quantile regression.

Chapter 2: Big Data

You are going to come to realize that big data is going to be the term that you are going to use for the data sets that are larger and more complex than the standard data processing application software is able to deal with. The challenges that come with big data are going to be the capturing of data, the visualization querying, sharing, transferring, data storage, data analysis, and the information privacy for the data that you are working with.

Big data applications

Big data has grown in its demand for information that different management specialists have needed in order to keep their business up and going. Some of these businesses are Microsoft, Dell, Software AG, Oracle Corporation and more. These companies have spent over fifteen billion dollars on software firms for the specialization of data management and analytics.

The big data business back in 2010 was worth over a hundred billion dollars and has continued to grow about 10%annually, which is two times faster than the software industry as a whole.

The government uses and adopts big data inside of their processes to allow for efficiencies in terms of innovation, productivity, and costs. However, this does not mean that there are not any flaws in the process of using big data. The use of data analysis is going to require several various parts of the government at once to work together and create the new processes that are needed in order to get the outcome that they are wanting.

United States of America

1. In 2012, the Obama administration said that in order to see how big data could help to address

some of the bigger issues that the government was dealing with, data research and development was going to be used.

2. It was big data that helped to get Barack Obama reelected to his presidency.

3. The federal government has six of the ten supercomputers that can be found in the world.

4. The National Security Agency built Utah data center and whenever they were done, they were able to handle massive amounts of data that was collected by the NSA over the world wide web. No one knows how much space there is for storing big data.

India

1. Big data helped to win the Indian general election that took place in 2014.

2. The government in India uses various techniques in order to ascertain exactly how the Indian electorate will respond to the government's actions.

United Kingdom

1. Big data for prescription drugs ties together the location, time, and origin of each prescription in their country. This helps to see what drugs are being used on the general patient.

2. Joining the data with the local authority about things like road gritting and meals on wheels services allows for the local authority to miss the weather-related delays that they have to watch out for.

International development

There has been research how effective big data can be used for ICT4D or the Information and Communication Technologies for Development. ICT4D proposes that big data does not only make a great improvement but also brings up some exceptional challenges when it comes to worldwide advancement.

There have been advancements in the analysis of big data which offers a more cost-effective opportunity so that it can improve the decision making that has to happen in the most critical development areas like health care, crime, and natural disaster.

On top of that, there has been data generated from users to offer new opportunities to those that are often unheard. But, there are some longstanding challenges that have appeared from the developing regions where there are inadequate technological infrastructures and human resources are limited.

Finance

Big data in finance is known as technical analysis. There are some nonfinancial data on the financial market which assists in making predictions known as alternative data. This means that the data that is non-financial is going to be what helps to make financial decisions because finances are going to affect more than just the economy and how it works.

Manufacturing

According to the TCS 2013 Global Trend Study, there have been some big improvements in supply planning and the quality of a product in order to provide the biggest benefit of big data that can be used for manufacturing.

A foundation for the transparency that is needed in the manufacturing industry has been provided by big data, which enables them to unravel the uncertainties like inconsistent component performance and the availability of a product.

So that it can be turned into useful data, the predictive manufacturing process has a near zero downtime and the transparency needs the advancement of prediction tools and a lot of data for a more systematic processing. This is an abstract structure for the predictive manufacturing that starts with the acquisition of data where there are diverse types of sensory data that are ready to obtain various voltage, pressure, acoustics, and more.

All of the historical data along with the sensory data will create the big data that is required in manufacturing. Whenever big data is generated, it is going to act as an input for the predictive tools and preventive strategies that you are going to use like Prognostics health management.

Cyber physical models

Currently, Prognostics health management uses data while they are working with it while allowing the analytical algorithms to perform the calculations so that they get more accurate results whenever there is enough information to input into the machine during its lifecycle. Some things that are going to be put in is the physical knowledge that someone knows or the system configurations.

Sometimes there has to be a systematic integrate so that data can be managed and analyzed before it is processed during the various stages that the machine is going to go through in its life cycle so that it can deal with data more effectively.

Whenever there is motivation, there is going to be a cyber physical model being developed because the model is going to be coupled with the motivation. Because of this coupled model, there is going to be a digital twin of the real machine that is going to operate in the cloud so that it can simulate the health conditions of the machine as well as the data that is inputted into it. This can best be described as a 5s systematic approach that is going to consist of the service, synthesis, synchronization, storage, and sensing of the data.

A digital image from the early design stage will be built by the model that is joined. During the product's design, the physical knowledge and system's information will be logged which is going to end up being based on the simulation model that is built as a reference for the future analysis.

There will be a generalization of the initial parameters which is going to make it to where they are turned into the data so it can be utilized for manufacturing or testing.

Health care

Big data analytics helps health care to improve by providing clinical risk interventions, waste and care reduction, and personalized medicine and prescriptive analysis. There are still some areas where improvements are going to be seen more than others because the improvement is going to be aspirational instead of implemented.

There are levels of data that is generated inside of the health care system and none of it is going to be trivial. The volume of the data that is coming in is going to continue to increase with the new adoptions of e-Health and m-Health (mobile health), and even wearable technology.

This makes it to where there is a greater need for those who can pay attention to this data and analyze it so that people are getting the best health care possible.

Education

There was a study conducted at McKinsey Global Institute that found there is a shortage of those who are trained to deal with big data by about one point five million people, this also includes the number of universities as well. This is why various universities such as UC Berkeley have created master's programs in order to train people to try and meet the demand that there is for big data.

There have even been private boot camps developed in order to help meet the demand.

Media

Big data is used in the media by showing those in media jobs what they should report on in order to reach their views and readers. However, there has been a shift in media where it appears to be moving away from the traditional approach of using newspapers and television shows. Now, they are going to social media and looking at what people are talking about and posting about. This is used so that they can target specific audiences with advertisements and articles that are found in the newspapers and magazines that are picked up by the consumer.

In fact, Channel 4 is a British public service television broadcaster and it is one of the biggest leaders in big data and data analysis.

Chapter 3: Data and Text Mining

Data mining is going to be the process of looking and discovering patterns in large sets of data by using methods that can be located at the intersection of statistics, database systems, and machine learning. This is an interdisciplinary subfield of computer science where the ultimate goal is to extract the information that is needed from a data set and then modify it so that it can be understood and used later.

There are at least six different classes that you are going to see in data mining.

1. Anomaly detection which is the detection of unusual data records. This is going to be where you are going to discover errors in your data which may end up causing you to have to look further into the error to see how you can change it and make your data produce the outcome that you are wanting.

2. Association rule learning is going to look for the various relationships that can be found between variables. Take for example how a store is going to obtain the various purchasing habits of a customer in order to learn which products they should keep in their store and what they can get rid of so they can bring in new products for their customers.

3. The cluster will be the task that you use in order to discover structures and groups inside of your data that are similar to each other without using any known structures in the data.

4. Classification will be when you generalize the structure that you know about so you can apply new data. Take for example how your email program is going to filter out your emails between legitimate and spam.

5. Regression, as we discussed earlier, is going to be the function that will model the data with the least errors that can be found all while estimating the relationships that can be found between the data and the data sets.

6. Summarization is going to give you some compact representation of the data set that you are working with. This is going to include the report generation.

Result validation

Even if you do not mean to, data mining can end up being misused which then can make results seem like they are significant, however, they cannot be reproduced onto a new sample of data because they are not going to actually predict the future behavior which means that they bare very little use. Many times, While not doing the accurate statistical hypothesis testing, the results, many times, are going to come from investigating too many hypotheses.

You can see a simple version of this in over fitting, however, the same problem has been known to arise during distinct phases of the process which can cause a split when applicable, test, or train, but it may not be enough to stop this from happening.

One of the final steps in knowledge discovery for over fitting is going to come from the data being able to verify which patterns have been created by the mining algorithms which can appear in the larger data set. You are going to have to use a test set for the data which your data mining algorithm is not going to be trained in order to overcome over fitting like this. The patterns that are learned are going to apply to the test set and going to result in an output that is going to be carried to the output that you were wanting.

Take for example a data mining algorithm that tries to tell the difference between spam emails and legitimate emails. This is going to be learned by the algorithm by using a training set of emails. After the algorithm has been trained to tell the difference, then its accuracy is going to be measured by how many emails are sent to the correct folder.

Standards

The standards needed for the data mining process have been tried to be defined by those who use data mining.

For instance, they released CRISP-DMor Cross Industry Standard Process for Data Mining back in '99, as well as in 2004 the Java Data Mining standard was put out there for the public to use in data analysis. These processes were made active in 2006 but have been stalled ever since because a final draft has not been reached.

The key is going to be Predictive Model Markup language in exchange for the extracted models like predictive analytics. The Data Mining Group developed this XML language. This language was supported as an exchange format by multiple data mining applications. It is only going to work with prediction models, just like the name suggests, where a certain data mining task has been set of great significance for applications in the business.

But, there are extensions that can be used to cover the subspace clustering having been proposed independent from the data mining group.

Notable uses

You are going to see data mining everywhere around you. Some of the biggest industries where you are going to see it is science and health care.

With science, it is obvious that data is going to be collected from the testing of hypotheses in order to make things better and more efficient. Such as, rocket fuel that is going to last longer and still get the shuttle to where its destination. Data is going to be collected from the various tests that are done on the various kinds of rocket fuel to see if it can be changed over to something that is more cost effective.

With health care, data is used to provide individualized health care to each person. This is done because not everyone is going to be coming in due to the fact that they have a sore throat. Not only that, but you cannot treat a heart attack or a stroke the same way that you would a gunshot wound. So, data has to be collected from the patient in order to give the best treatment that there is.

Privacy concerns and ethics

Even though the actual term data mining is not going to have any ethical implications it is still often referred to as the mining of information that relates to people's behavior.

The ways that the information from data mining is used has caused privacy concerns as well as ethics and legality issues to be brought up. One of the biggest concerns is how the data from data mining is being used by the commercial data sets or the government for things like law enforcement purposes or for the national security.

Data mining brings up the need for data preparation which has the possibility of uncovering information or patterns that can end up compromising the privacy obligations and confidentiality. Using data aggregation is one way for this to possibly happen. The aggregation of data is going to involve combining the data together in such a way that it is going to facilitate an analysis.

Data aggregation is not necessarily data mining, but as a result of the preparation of data before and the purpose of that data, it can cause a threat to one's privacy once all the data has been compiled because the miner now has access to the new data set and is going to be able to pick out specific pieces of information whereas before the data left the user anonymous.

That is why it is endorsed that people should be informed of what the data is going to going to be used for before the data is even collected.

Text mining

Also known as text data mining, text mining is going to be equivalent to text analytics. It typically involves structuring the input and finding the patterns inside of that structured data before interpreting the output. Text mining is the method of getting high-quality information from a proved text. High-quality in text mining is going to refer to the combination of the novelty, most relevant, and most appealing in the text. The high-quality information is going to be pulled from the constructing of trends and patterns through things like statistical pattern learning.

Text analysis involves the lexical analysis used to study the recognizing patterns, the word frequency distributions, so on and so forth and the retrieval of information. The overarching goal is going to be to take that text and turn it into data for analysis through the application of natural language processing and analytical methods.

Text analysis processes

There are subtasks that you are going to use in the larger text analytics such as:

1. Identification of corpus or the retrieval of information. This is a preparatory step which you are going to use to identify of gather the set of textual materials that are found inside of a file system or on the internet.

2. Because some text analytics systems are going to implement exclusively to more advanced statistical methods where others are going to implement more expanded analysis.

3. The named entity recognition will be used for the gazetteers or the statistical technique in order to identify the named text features such as names, symbols so on and so forth. disambiguation is going to use contextual clues that may end up being required in order to decide what the text is referring to.

4. Recognition of pattern identified entities are going to be features like email addresses or phone numbers which can be determined through similarity of patterns or common expressions.

5. The Noun phrases and other terms that can all point to the same object will be identified by the co-reference.

6. The relationships and facts extraction are going to identify the associations through the entities found in the text.

7. Sentiment analysis is going to include the discerning subjective material as well as the extracting of various forms of attitudinal information. The text analytics techniques for this are going to assist in analyzing the sentiment pointed at the entity.

8. Quantitative text analysis will be the set of techniques that are used but they are going to be stemmed from the social sciences wherein a computer or a human is going to extract the semantic or grammatical connections between words to discover the meaning of the stylistic arrangement for a casual personal text for things such as psychological profiling.

Applications

With technology as advanced as it is, it works not just for private use, but for the government, research and even the needs of businesses. The applications can be sorted into categories and then analyzed by type or function. If you use this approach, then you can classify solutions. Some of the application categories may be things like:

1. Social media monitoring
2. Enterprise business intelligence and data mining
3. Search and informative access
4. E-discovery and records management
5. Automated ad placement
6. Publishing
7. National security and intelligence
8. Publishing

And so much more.

Security applications

A lot of the text mining software packages are marketed to those who use security applications for things like monitoring or analysis of the internet for national security purpose. This is also going to work for the encryption and decryption of files.

Biomedical applications

There are a lot of different applications that are going to be used for text mining when it comes to biomedical literature. One application that you can find online is going to be known as PubGene. This application is going to combine the biomedical text mining with the visualization of the network on an internet service.

If you are searching for biomedical texts, a search engine known as GoPubMed can be used.

Software applications

The software and method that you use for text mining are going to be developed and researched by some of the bigger firms such as Microsoft so that they can further automate the processes and work in different areas of searching and indexing so that the results are improved.

An effort has been placed on creating software in the public sector so that terroristic activities can be monitored and tracked which is important to stop and intercept terrorist attacks.

Online media applications

Many large media companies like the Tribune company is using text mining for them to be able to gather information from their readers and this information will then be used to improve search experiences. This, in turn, increases the site's revenue and a lot of readers stick around because of the relevance of the search results.

An added plus is that the editors are able to package and share news through features that are going to increase the opportunities to monetize content that is placed on their site.

In making their site more effective, they are going to obtain more readers because they know what their readers want to see.

Business and marketing applications

Text mining is used for customer relationship management and marketing. Text mining is used to improve the predictive analytics models for customer attribution. It can also be applied to the stock returns predictions.

Sentiment analysis

This type of analysis is going to include analysis of things such as movie reviews so that it can be estimated on how favorable a review is going to be for a movie. Analysis such as this can end up needed in labeling the sentiment of the words used and even being part of a labeled data set. Resources for the sentiment of concepts and words will be made for concept net and word net.

The text is going to be used to catch emotions in affective computing. The text will be based on the various approaches that affective computing has used in things like news stories and student evaluations.

Academic applications

One of the issues for text mining is how important it is to publishers who have a large database of information that needs to be indexed. This is going to be especially true when it comes to scientific disciplines where there are highly specific pieces of information inside of the text. So, initiatives are going to be taken like nature's proposal for an interface that allows for open text mining.

Some of the academic institutions that have become involved with text mining are:

1. The National center for text mining which was the first publicly funded text mining center in the entire world. This center is operated by the University of Manchester as well as the Tsujii lab from the University of Tokyo. These two collectives are creating customized tools and research facilities that are going to offer advice to the academic community. They are funded by the joint information systems committee as well as the United Kingdom research councils. The main focus is on text mining inside of

biomedical and biological sciences. However, the research continues to expand into areas like social sciences.

2. In the United States, you are going to find the school of information located at the University of California where a program is being developed called BioText so that biology researchers can use text mining and its analysis.

3. The text analysis portal for research is housed at the University of Alberta and has a scholarship project to work on the newest text analysis applications while creating a gateway for researchers who are new to the practice to be able to work with it.

Chapter 4: Data Management

Data management is going to be all of the disciplines that you use to manage data so that it is a valuable resource.

There is a foundation in Europe known as the European Foundation for Quality Management as well as the Competence Center Corporate Data Quality that says corporate data quality management is the complete set of activities that you are going to use to improve the quality of your data both preventive and reactive. One of the main premises for this is the business relevance of high-quality data at the corporate level. Some of the activities you may use for high-quality data will be.

1. Strategy for corporate data quality. Here different business drivers are going to be affected and there are going to be multiple divisions inside of an organization that work on it together. All in all, every department in a company needs to work together to ensure that

they are working with the highest quality of data.

2. Corporate data quality controlling. There has to be a strict policy to monitor the data according to the company's policies, standards, and procedures. Any changes in the compliance of the data should be reported to the stakeholders.

3. Corporate data quality organization will be where the roles and responsibilities are defined so that everyone knows what they are expected to do with the data that they are working with.

4. To handle the data properly and in a standardized way and to ensure the data quality, corporate data quality processes and methods are put into place throughout the entire company. Standard procedures and guidelines must be put into place in the company's daily processes.

5. Data architecture for corporate data quality. The architecture of the data is going to be the model that you are using which will be made up of the models that are used for corporate data

and the storage of that data along with how it is distributed.

6. Applications for corporate data quality will include the software applications that are used to support the activities mentioned above. Any software that is used has to be monitored, managed, and improved upon continuously.

Data management is also going to be included in managing the databases that your data is being stored on. You will have to clean out the database and make sure that it has enough space on it to hold all of the data that you are working with. Not only that, you are also going to have to ensure that it has been updated and only those that need to get into the database have access to it. This is going to prevent people from getting a hold of data that they should not have access to.

Which leads us to the security of that data. You have to ensure that your data is protected completely due to the fact that you may be working with data that is sensitive. Take for example, if you are working in a doctor's office. The data that you are working with is going to consist of people's social security numbers, birthdays, and health issues. If someone was to get a hold of that, not only would they be able to steal someone's identity, but they could sell the information online.

Therefore, you have to make sure that you have passwords and that files are encrypted whenever they are sent between workers so that if it does fall into the wrong hands, it is not going to be easily accessed. Along with that, but you are going to know whenever someone tries to get the data because you will receive an alert that someone is trying to access it with the incorrect password.

Now, what do you do with data that you no longer need? The retention policy for your company is going to vary depending on where you work, but just because data is no longer needed does not mean that you can just delete it. There are going to be rules that you are going to have to follow in order to discard of the data in a safe way so that personal and confidential information that is listed in that data is not freely given to someone who may be going through the trash or gets your computer whenever you upgrade.

If you are working with paper then the best thing that you can do is mark out all of the data that no one needs to have and then shred it. You can do the same thing on your computer by placing a shredding program on the computer. You will need to speak to your company's IT department about this before you do it.

Managing your data is also going to include how you put it onto paper so that those who are using the data to make decisions can see it in an obvious way rather than having to try and locate what they are looking for. Below is one of the best ways that you can manage your data in an organized fashion not only for you but for those using it to make decisions that could affect your job.

Decision tree

Your decision tree will be the tool that you are going to use whenever you need support in the decisions that you are making. The decision tree is called a tree because it looks like a tree of your decisions and outcomes have been listed. This is another way that you can display algorithms that were used in the analysis process

Decision trees will be used when working with operations research, or more specifically, whenever the decision report that you do needs to identify the strategies that were used so that you could reach that goal. But, you are going to find it is more popular when dealing with machine learning.

When it comes time to think about the decision tree, you should think of it like a flow chart where all of the nodes and tests that are run can be placed so that you can show the result of each test. With decision analysis, the decision tree is going to be used as an influence diagram that you will apply when you are using visual tools for the values that you expect and any alternatives that have been collected.

Most of the decision trees that you work with are going to have at least three nodes.

1. End nodes: These are typically going to be triangles. These are the final result of that decision.
2. Decision nodes: The squares that are on your tree that are going to show choices that you can choose from.
3. Chance nodes: These nodes are going to be shown by circles on your tree. The chance nodes are the ones that show what happens if you take the path instead of a different one.

Your tree will be used in research that is done by operations along with management for those operations. Usually, the decisions are going to be online and there will not be any recall under the data that comes back as incomplete. Decision trees have to show the parallelism between probability models and the best choice for the algorithm that should be used inside of that model. You can also use a tree for calculating conditional probabilities.

Tree elements

When you look at a decision tree, you are going to read it left to right just like you would anything else. There are going to be burst nodes on the tree, but there will not be any sink nodes. So, when created manually, a tree can get enormous due to the fact that someone is manually drawing the tree and adding the nodes that need to be added.

Decision rules

A lot of decision trees will be linearized with rules of the decision so that your outcomes are in the left node and the conditions are going to follow will conjoin with an if clause. Your rules are usually going to come in this form.

If (condition 1) and (condition 2) and (condition 3) then (the outcome)

Your decision rules will be created by the rules of association where the variable for your target is listed on the right. Decision rules are also going to show temporal or causal relations on your tree.

Decision tree with symbols

You may find your decision tree looks a lot like a flow chart and contains symbols that are used in order to make it easier for the person making the decision to understand and read the data and make an informed decision

Rule induction

Decision trees can also be seen as generative models based on the rules that come from empirical data. These trees are going to be used in order to define the various accounts of data all while attempting to minimize the number of levels that are shown on the tree.

Chapter 5: Data Reduction and Clustering

Data reduction is known as the transformation of digital information derived empirically or experimentally into the corrected and most simple form possible. One of the basic concepts of reduction is to take the data down to the most meaningful parts.

Whenever information is pulled from readings off of a machine there is going to be a transformation period where it is taken from analog and placed into digital form. When the data is already in digital form, then the reduction is going to be when you go in and edit it so that you can create a tabular summary.

Whenever observations are kept discrete, then the underlying phenomenon is continuous then you are going to have to use interpolation and smoothing. Most of the time, data reduction is going to be used to find the measurement errors. There are some ideas that the errors are going to be needed before the value can be determined.

Take for example those who work in astronomy have to reduce the data from the satellites that are constantly recording data so that we can discover new worlds. If they did not reduce the data, then we would be going through thousands of megabytes of data which could cause us to miss out on learning something new.

There is even some research going on about reducing data that comes off of wireless devices that are used for monitoring health and making a diagnosis.

Reducing data may seem like a lot of work, but in the end, it is going to be helpful because you are going to be able to locate the data that you need to work with instead of trying to work with all of the data that is within your grasp. Not only that, but you are going to be reducing costs because you are only going to be working with the data that you absolutely need.

To top it off you are going to be doing your job more effectively since you are not going to be wasting your time with data that is useless, but you are going to be making yourself valuable to your boss because you are not going to be going to them with information that is going to place your project back. Instead, you will be presenting accurate data in a way that just leaves the decision-making process to them.

Reducing data is also going to assist you in getting rid of duplicate data that you are not going to need, therefore you are going to combine data so that it lessens the load of data that you are working with. Along with this, you are going to be opening up storage for more data which is going to make it to where you are not constant deleting data.

Whenever you reduce data, you will be able to see what is missing and if you really need to obtain that piece of data. Along those lines, when you are only getting the data that is missing, you are reducing your workload since you are not going to be having to redo your investigation going through and getting all of the data once more.

When it comes to creating visualizes having reduced data will make your visual smaller and easier to follow. This is going to make your life easier because you are not going to have to worry about trying to figure out how to present the data and how to make it to where people can follow the data in a way that they can understand it.

Another wonderful thing about reducing your data is that you are not going to have as many tests to run to prove your hypothesis.

Best practices

These are some of the most common techniques used for data reduction

1. Order the data by size
2. Give a brief summary of the data
3. Table diagonalization where all of the rows and columns for the table is reorganized to make the patterns easier to discover.

4. Take out the chart junk like pictures and extra lines

5. Round to at least one or two of the most effective digits. The effective digits are going to be the ones that vary as part of the data that is being used.

6. Use a layout that is easy to follow and labels so that the person looking at the chart knows where to look next.

7. Use averages in order to provide a visual focus just like the summary.

Data clustering

Clustering is the task of grouping objects in a way that they fall into the same group. These objects are going to be similar in nature. The main task for exploratory data mining and statistical data analysis is to use things like image analysis, information retrieval so on and so forth.

Cluster analysis is not going to work on one specific algorithm, but the general task is going to end up being solved through various algorithms that are going to differ in their notion of what constitutes a cluster and exactly how efficient it is.

There are some popular notions for clusters that are going to include small distances that fall between the cluster members and dense area of data space. Clustering is going to be formulated as a multi objective optimization problem. There is going to be an appropriate clustering algorithm along with parameter settings which are going to depend on the individual data sets and how the results are going to be used.

Connectivity based clustering

This clustering method is going to also be known as hierarchical clustering which is going to be based on the core idea of the objects being related to objects that are nearby than objects that are further apart. With this algorithm, the objects are going to be connected to create clusters based on how far apart they are.

Clusters are going to be described the maximum distance needed to connect the parts of the cluster.

Centroid based clustering

With this algorithm, the clusters will be represented by a central vector that is not going to necessarily be a member of that data set. Whenever the number of clusters is fixed to k. k is going to be defined as an optimization problem where you will find k cluster centers and then assign those objects to the nearest cluster center which is going to square the distances from the cluster so they are minimized.

The approach of NP-hard, which is the known optimization problem, is going to search for the approximate solutions. This is often referred to as the k means algorithm, and also known as Lloyd's algorithm method.

Distribution based clustering

In this clustering model, it is going to be related to the statistics that you find in distribution models. The objects that belong to the same distribution are known as clusters. Resembling the way that artificial data sets are generated through a random sampling of objects from the distribution is one of the convenient properties of this approach.

As this is a theoretical foundation of the model, they are going to suffer from the problem of over fitting unless you put constraints on the model's complexity. The more complex that the model is, the better the data will be explained.

Data based clustering

The clusters are going to be described as the areas that are made of higher density than those left over in the data set with density based clustering. Separate clusters are going to be required by the objects inside of the sparse areas; they are usually treated to be border points and noise.

DBSCAN is known as one of the more common density based clustering methods. There are some newer methods that are going to be defined as density reachability. Some are similarly linked to based clustering which is based on the connecting of points that are inside of some certain distance points. But, it is only connecting points, that are going to satisfy the density criterion that was stated in the original variant as defined by the least number of other objects that sit inside of the radius. The cluster is going to be consistent with all the density connected objects as well as the objects that are inside of that object's range.

Another property of the DBSCAN is going to be that it is not as complex as you may think it would be. It is going to require a linear number of ranged queries that are in the database and it is going to be discovered with the same results.

The biggest drawback to DBSCAN is going to be that it will expect a density drop in order to detect the cluster borders. On most data sets, there is going to be some overlapping Gaussian distributions which are going to be a common use when it comes to artificial data. The clusters borders are going to be produced by the algorithms.

Chapter 6: Web Scraping

When you scrape data that will be utilized for the obtaining data from websites, that is called as web scraping. By searching in a web browser or by using hypertext transfer protocol, web scraping software can be found. As you web scrap, it will have to be done manually by the user of the software. In other words, you will be copying text off of the internet and place it into a database or spreadsheet for analysis or retrieval at a later date.

Web scraping on a web page means that you are going to be calling the web page and then pulling information from it. The fetching of a page means that you are going to be downloading it which your computer browser is going to do whenever you are viewing it. Once that is done, web crawling will be used as the main component for web scraping in which you are going to fetch pages to process later. After the fetching is completed, then the extraction process is going to take place. The page's content will be searched and modified as the data is copied over to a spreadsheet.

Web scraping is going to usually start by taking something off of a web page in order to use it somewhere else, for instance, you would be taking phone numbers and name of companies that you are going to call later.

Techniques

Web scraping is a process that is going to occur automatically whenever you are mining data. The only thing is that you are going to be getting everything off of the internet exclusively. Most of the time it is going to be the interactions between humans and computers. All of the current web scraping solutions are going to range from humans taking care of the scraping to systems being automated in able to convert an entire website into a structured information that has limitations.

Human copy and paste

There are going to be times that the best web scraping technology is not going to be good enough to do what it is that you are wanting to do, therefore it makes a human's manual examination the best solution. Not just that, but there are times that this is going to be the only solution whenever there are barriers set up by websites to stop machine automation.

Text pattern matching

Another easy but equally as effective approach in getting data from a web page is to use the UNIX grep command to find patterns while facilitating programming languages such as Python or Perl.

HTTP programming

The web pages that are static or dynamic can be pulled through the posting of HTTP requests through the remote web server by using socket programming.

HTML parsing

There are a lot of websites that have an enormous collection of pages that are generated dynamically with an underlying structured source such as a database. The data is going to be in the same category and is usually going to be encoded through similar pages by a common template or script.

When data mining, the program is going to detect a template from the proper information source to pull the content and then translate it into a more relational form known as the wrapper.

The wrapper is going to create algorithms that are going to assume the input pages for the wrapper will induction systems so it can conform to the template that they identified in turns of the URL's common scheme.

DOM parsing

Whenever a website is embedded in a web browser like Mozilla Firefox, the browser control will determine on if the program can retrieve the dynamic content that is generated on the client side of the script.

Browsers such as these are going to control the parse web pages inside of a DOM tree which is going to be based on the programs that are used to retrieve parts of the web pages.

Vertical aggregation

There are a few companies that are developing vertical specific harvesting platforms. These platforms are going to be used to create and monitor the massive number of bots that are being used for specific verticals inside of the no man in the loop – there is no direct human involvement – which means that there is no work related to the targeted site.

There is some preparation involved which is going to mean that you have to establish a knowledge base for the entire vertical and then the platform will end up creating a lot to do the work for you.

Semantic annotation recognizing

There are pages that you may scrap that will embrace the metadata, the semantic markups, and the annotations in order to locate specific pieces of data. Should the annotations be embedded in the pages like Microformat does, then this technique is going to be seen as a special case for the DOM parsing.

In other words, the annotations are going to be organized, stored, and managed apart from the web pages in order for you to obtain the data before the page is scraped.

Computer version web page analysis

There are going to be some efforts that are going to use machine learning as well as computer versions in order to try and identify the exact information from web pages through the interpretation of the page like a human may do.

Software

The software tools that are made available for you to web scrap can be customized for the web scraping solutions that you need. It is this software that will attempt to automatically figure out the data structure for the page or provide the recording interface that is going to remove the necessity that is there to manually write out the web scraping code or other scripting functions that are going to be used to extract and transform the content in the databases interface that will end up being stored in a database.

There are some web scraping software that will be used in order to extract data from the API.

Some examples of the tools that you may use are:

1. URL is a command line tool that contains a library that can be used to transfer the data inside of a URL to support a wide range of http methods such as GET and POST.

2. Diffbot will use a computer version to automatically extract the data from a web page through the interpretation of pages visually just like a human would.

3. Data toolbar is an add on that you can use with web browsers such as Google Chrome,Mozilla Firefox, and Internet Explorer to collect data that is structured from that web page and convert it into a tabular format that will then be entered into a database or spreadsheet.

4. Heritrix will obtain the pages and then use a web crawler to design a web archiving that is written by the internet archive.

5. HTML unit will take a headless browser so that it can retrieve web pages for web scraping and more.

6. Imacros is an extension for the browser that you use in order to record code, share it, and replay the browser automation.

JavaScript

1. jQuery
2. Grease monkey
3. Node.js
4. phantomJS

SaaS version

1. fscraper
2. import.io
3. uScraper

Web crawling framework

This framework is going to be used in order to build web scrapers that you are going to have the option of using.

If this is the option that you are wanting, then you will use Scrapy.

Preventing web scraping

There are tools that the administrators of websites can use to slow down or even stop bots from scraping their website.

1. Block IP address. This can be done manually or based on criteria that you set up for your website like geolocation and DNSRBL. In doing this you are going to be blocking all of the devices that browser from that IP address.

2. Disable the web services API so that the website's system is not exposed.

3. There are some bots that are going to say who they are through user agent strings. You have the option of blocking based on this such as robots that use text like google bot. There are other bots that are going to not make a distinction between them or a human that is

using the browser so it may be harder to tell the difference so that you can block them.

4. Bots can be blocked through the monitoring of excessive traffic that your web page sees.

5. There are some bots that are going to be easier to be blocked with the tools that you are using due to the fact that you can make it to where you can verify if a real person is using the site through Captchas. Bots are not always going to be coded to get past some of the captcha patterns or they may even employ a third-party service to get a human to get past the captcha challenges before taking over once more. This is how some sites are scraped despite the fact that they use devices to stop bots.

Chapter 7: Data Analysis in the Real World

There are risks that you have to know about in order to be able to do data analytics properly in order to protect yourself, your company, and your data.

1. Data security

Security is going to be the first thing that anyone thinks of when it comes to dealing with businesses and people who are working with data. They are not going to want another company to get a hold of data that they can use to bet you out on something new that you are trying to put out. At the point in time that data is taken from a big company, it makes news and is not forgotten due to the fact that it opens the public's eyes to how easily other people can get a hold of their data. The more data that a company has, the bigger target they make themselves.

2. Data privacy

It is not going to matter what type of data is being used, it has to be protected and the privacy should be kept to those who absolutely need to know about the information. The less information that is told to those who do not need to know it, the less risk you are going to be opening yourself up to.

3. Costs

There are going to be costs that are going to be associated with the collection of data, however, there are also going to be costs for storing and analyzing the data as well. Then you have to throw in the compliance costs that you will have to pay so that you can avoid issues that are going to be associated with your data.

It is at this point that you are going to need to get rid of data that is not needed so that you can save some money and time not having to go through unnecessary procedures.

4. Bad analytics

This occurs whenever you misinterpret the data that you are analyzing. In the event that you draw links between the various parts of data is going to be a coincidence. The data that you work with from something big, you are going to be able to draw some links, but that does not mean that the links that you can draw are going to be correct.

5. Bad data

Sometimes there will be a collection of data that is not going to be worth anything. Bad data is collected when you do not have enough time to gather the appropriate data for the study that you are conducting. This can hurt your company due to the fact that you are going to have to take the time once again to get a hold of the data that you need or you will have to put out a product without the proper data which can harm sales in your company.

Real world examples

You can easily say that data analysis happens in the real world, but how are you going to know what to look for if you do not have a few examples. In this section, we are going to discuss how you can spot real world examples of the data analysis.

Video streaming services

When it comes to video streaming services you can watch entire videos online without having to wait for the next episode to air. But, the service is collecting data from you as you watch.

Depending on what you are watching and how you rate them is going to tell the service what recommendations it should give you thanks to the data that it is analyzing. This also helps to tell them what to keep on their site and off their site.

Ancestors

Some websites allow for you to find out more about your family all by placing a few facts about yourself and your family into the website. The more information that you want, the more information that you are going to have to put in.

The data that you place into their system is going to be sent out the database and analyzed in order to match it up with other records that have data that you are looking for. The data is going to be analyzed carefully in order to make sure that you are not paired up with incorrect family records.

Medical research

Medical research is not always going to occur on a human being. There are times that it is going to happen on a strain of bacteria as the doctor doing the research is attempting to figure out how to cure a disease or figure out how to knock out something like the common cold.

This data is going to be extracted from the study and analyzed to see if it works or not. If it does not work then they are going to continue with their research.

One example is the study of the E. Coli strain to see if the doctor could figure out how to kill the strain with the proper mix of antibiotics.

Weather

There is an independent system operator that you can find in California that helps over thirty-five million customers get their power. The software that the ISO uses is going to collect data points to ensure that the power is still on and look at weather so that if the power goes out, they can work to get it fixed as fast as possible.

This is also going to be similar to a water company in Ontario that provides water for residences and businesses.

Infusion pumps

It is important to know that when it comes to infusions, doctors and nurses do not need to go chasing an infusion pump down when they need it. There is software being used in one hospital that keeps track of how the patient is doing on their infusion which assists the doctor in figuring out if the infusion is working for the patient or not.

Vegas

The machines that you see in Vegas are going to collect data. If there are not many people playing that slot machine, then that machine is taken out and another is put in its place. This is done so that their profits continue to go through the roof.

Conducting data analysis

Here is where you are going to get a more broken-down version of what data analysis truly is.

Organize your data

1. When using an electronic database, you need to organize your data. Whenever placing this data in the database, you have to make sure that all of the data is going to the proper place. There are applications such as excel that you can use in order to organize the data in a spreadsheet that will enable you to search the data quickly.

2. Put your responses into digital form. If you have conducted a survey, then you will take the answers to that survey and count them out so that you can look at how many answered that question that specific way.

3. You are going to organize your data by age or gender depending on how it best works for that study.

4. Check for mistakes, you do not want your work to be filled with mistakes or else your work is not going to be accurate.

Statistical tests

1. T tests are some of the most common tests that are going to be run on the data that you are working in order to find the average of the samples that have been collected.

2. You can also run an ANOVA test to compare the means of multiple groups. This is a powerful test to find out the differences in your comparisons.

3. Linear regression is going to help you to see the variances depending on what the dependent variable is. Whenever you use linear regression, you will be measuring the association between two variables and how clear the connection is.

4. Your ANCOVA test can be used by taking two regression lines and comparing them such as ages or genders.

Analyzing the data

1. Ensure that your question is defined. You are not going to want a study question that is impossible to answer.

2. Talk to a statistician to get their help with the statistics. Working with statistics can be hard and the more data that you are working with, the more complex it is going to be. However, a statistician is going to be able to analyze the data and tell you exactly which tests to run in order to get you the results that you are wanting. They also can look at the data after it has been collected and let you know if it was tested properly or not.

3. Pick the statistical test that you are wanting to run and run it. You will need to find some program like SAS or R that you can use to execute the test. So, keep in mind that if you

use a program, you are going to need some programming experience to make sure that you are running the test properly.

Chapter 8: Social Network Analysis

The process that you use in order to investigate the social structures through the use of networks and graph theory is called social network analysis. Through social network analysis, the network structures in terms of nodes that are connected to them are going to be characterized. Some examples would be to visualize social media networks, friendships, and sexual relationships. Social network analysis came up as a method to modern sociology and has acquired a compelling following in other studies.

Metrics

Homophily is going to extend to which actors will form times with those that are similar versus the dissimilar ones. Similarities are going to be defined by race and age. This is also referred to assortativity.

The number of content forms that are contained inside of a tie will be shown by multiplexity. For instance, two people who are working together but they are friends which give them a multiplexity of two.

Mutuality/reciprocity the extent is going to show how two actors are going to interact with each other.

Propinquity is the tendency for actors to have ties that are geographically close to others.

Network closure is the measure of completeness for relational triads such as a person's friends who are friends with those friends. This would be called a transitivity.

Distributions

An individual's weak ties that will fill a structural hole which is going to provide a link between two people is known as the bridge. It is also going to be the shortest route whenever the longer one is not possible because of the elevated risk of distortion.

Density is the portion of direct ties inside of the network which relates to the total number possible.

Centrality will refer to a group of metrics that is going to quantify the importance of a node inside of the network.

Distance is the least amount of ties that is required between two people.

Tie strength will define the linear combination of reciprocity, intimacy, and time. The stronger the ties are associated to propinquity, transitivity, and homophily. The weaker ties are tied to the bridges.

Structural holes show the absence of ties between two distinct parts of a network. You will be able to find and exploit the structural holes that can give someone a competitive advantage. This concept is often referred to as the alternative conception of social capital and was developed by an American sociologist, Ronald Burt.

Segmentation

The groups are going to be called cliques in which each person is tied to directly. These social circles are going to be less stringency of direct contact which is going to imprecise the blocks in the event that precision is wanted.

Clustering coefficients are going to be the measure of the likelihood of two associated nodes. The higher the clustering coefficient will indicate the greater cliquishness.

The degree in which people are connected directly to each other by cohesive bonds will be shown by cohesion. The structural cohesion is going to relate to the least number of people who would be considered to be disconnected from the group.

Models and visualization

When it comes to the network data, it is necessary to know about the visual representation of the social network and it will show you the results of the analysis. There are many methods that you can use to show the data that is obtained by social network analysis. Modules that you can use for network visualization can be found in most of the analytic software.

Exploration of the data will be made by the displaying nodes and tie into other layouts while attributing to size, color, and other properties that you are going to find out about the nodes. The visual representations of the networks are going to be powerful methods used for conveying the complexity of the information, however, it will end up to misrepresenting the structural properties in order to capture a quantitative analysis if interpreting the node and the graph's properties for the visual displays alone will not be done carefully.

There are signed graphs that are going to show you both the good and the bad relationships that occur between humans. One of the positive edges is between two nodes will denote a positive relationship while the negative between the nodes is going to show you the negative in a relationship.

Signed social networks are going to have unbalanced and balanced cycles. Balanced cycles are going to be cycles where the products are positive. A group of people who probably are not going to change their opinions about the other people in the group are going to be represented by the balanced graphs according to a balanced theory.

A group of people who are going to change their opinion of those in the group will be shown in unbalanced graphs.

Social network analysis will be used as a tool to facilitate change by showing different approaches of participatory network mapping. Those that participate in your study are going to give you the data that you need to map out a network as you conduct your study. One example of this is to take a pen and paper to your session and show how each person is perceived through influences and goals that they have in their careers.

Being able to collect qualitative data and then figure out how to ask clear questions all the while making sure that the network data is collected properly is one benefit that you are going to discover.

Networking potential

Social networking potential is going to be a numeric coefficient that is derived through the use of algorithms. To represent the size of someone's social network and how they can influence that network, these algorithms are going to be used. There are two primary functions for the social networking potential coefficients.

1. How people are classified based on their social networking potentials.

2. The weights of the respondents in quantitative marketing research studies

When you calculate the social network potential of those that are in your study, you can target high social networking potential respondents as well as the relevance and strength of the marketing research that is going to drive the viral marketing strategies to be improved.

Variables can be used to determine a person's social networking potential which is going to include those who are participating, their activities, group memberships, recognition, leadership roles, and how they contribute to non- electronic media as well as the past distribution of information inside of their network.

The acronym for social networking potential as well as the first algorithms that were developed to help quantify to a person's social networking potential was first described in the white paper "Advertising Research is Changing" which was published in 2003.

The very first book was written to discuss how Alpha users work among mobile telecoms audiences according to 3G marketing by Ahonen Kasper and Melkko in '04.

Practical applications

Social network analysis can be utilized thoroughly in a great extent of disciplines and applications. There are some common network applications which include mining, data aggregation, network modeling, network propagation, network modeling, behavior analysis and sampling.

Businesses in the private sector use the social network to support activities like analysis and customer interactions, marketing demands and business intelligence. There are some public sectors that are using it as well in order to develop leader engagement strategies to analyze the community-based problem solving and group or individual engagement for media use.

The social network analysis will also be used for intelligence activities. Techniques such as this are going to allow for the analysts to map an undercover or underground organization like an intelligence ring or a street gang. The NSA uses it to do analysis tests on terrorist cells or other networks that seem like they are a threat to national security.

So, in other words, social network analysis is going to show you the relationships that you are going to find between people. This does not have to be how they put their personal life out on social media, but how they work together. There is no escaping the negative relationships because they are a part of life, but they can be used to analyze and figure out how to prevent those negative relationships from happening to other people.

The positive relationships are going to be used to figure out how you can promote other healthy and positive relationships amongst people which are going to help create those positive ties with other people.

These ties are going to show you how other people tie to each other in such a way that you are going to be able to figure out how everyone works together in the world and how human interaction is important.

Chapter 9: Data Analysis Techniques

1. Develop the questions that need to be researched and link them to a study that you are able to design

Data is going to be collected to answer a question. The question should be able to answer a question in a way that it can be tested in a study so that you can take the data that you collect and analyze it in order to make sure you make your boss and customer happy.

These studies are going to answer questions or be experiments that you can conduct. The case studies will give you a plethora of information that is going to assist in making you company go further in a more productive manner. You should keep these three things in mind when it comes to your question.

> a. Is your question well-articulated?
> b. Is your question able to be answered with the resources and time limit that you are working against?
> c. Is your question a good fit with the study that you are conducting?

Whenever you are planning the research that you are going to be doing, you are going to want to ensure that you have a clear purpose as to what it is that you are trying to accomplish and the questions we listed above are going to help make sure that happens.

You are going to want to discover a few different study objectives to show you a variety of data for you to analyze.

You will want to collect and analyze the qualitative data that has been collected.

Four different uses for collecting data are:

1. Individual interviews: these are going to be discussions that occur between at least two different people and are going to have some sort of structure to them as well as a purpose that is trying to be met. The interviewer is going to be trying to get any knowledge or perspective that the interviewee has on the topic that is being investigated. This is usually done in an effort to get additional facts from that individual to learn more about the topic that is at hand.

2. Focus group discussions: focus groups are typically groups that are organized and are going to consist of six to eight different people discussing the topic that is being researched. As the people discuss the issue at hand, they are going to be able to agree and disagree with each other and the opinions that are being put before them to address based on their own beliefs and experiences. The people that you choose for the focus group need to be relevant

to what it is that you are trying to study and make sure that you inform the participants about everything that they are going to be discussing. You will want to recruit people that are going to give you a good representation of the population that you are targeting.

3. Photo voice: this method is going to allow for a person to identify and help improve their community, life, or engage in a program through the use of photography and captions that go with that photograph. Photo voice is going to enable the group of people participating to have access to a camera that is going to allow them to discuss and share stories that are going to be significant to what you are studying.

4. Picture story: This method is going to be aimed mostly at children so that they are able to participate in the study in a fun way that is going to be geared towards their learning level. These pictures are going to be pictures that they draw or stories that they tell depending on how old they are and where their level of

literacy lies. This is typically an inexpensive research method that is going to get the views of the child on what they are being asked.

When it comes to the samples of those that may participate in your study, you are going to use at least one of these methods.

1. Random purposeful sampling: this sampling is going to be purposeful, and the group will be primarily made up of random participants.
2. Extreme or typical sampling: you will learn about the strange or the standard tests such as those who have gone through the struggle that you are studying.
3. Snowball sampling: you will ask multiple people to point out others who can be interviewed as well due to the fact that they are open and contain some kind of understanding of the issue you are studying.

2. Qualitative data analysis

The data analysis is going to be whenever you take the data that has been collected reduced down to the amounts that make sense while ensuring that you have something from all of the sources that have participated in your study. The impressions that are gathered will shed light and answer the question that you wanted to answer.

Using this process means that you are going to be taking the information that is the most descriptive information to find out the explanation or interpretation of what information you have gathered.

Just like was discussed earlier, you are going to want to make sure that you are cleaning up your data so that you do not have to worry about working with data that is not useful or is going to negate your research.

Qualitative analysis will end up paying special attention to the words that come out of people's mouths so that you can attempt to figure out if there is any contradiction to the research or to show a theme or trend that can emerge from the data that you have collected.

When it comes to analyzing your data, you will have to reduce the data to the data that only falls inside of the framework so that they can help you get to your object, all while falling inside of the policy that was set into place when you first formed your question.

When it comes to reducing your data, you will be looking for answers that keep to the topic of your question that you are attempting to answer. This is going to be the cleaning process that was discussed earlier in the book.

Many in data analysis recommend that you take a more exploratory perspective in order to look at any new impressions that are going to assist in shaping your interpretation and finding things that you did not see before. While you code your data, you are going to see some abstract themes most likely that are going to appear in the data that has been coded. You are going to also see links between the codes that have been created which is going to bring out more information that will hopefully support your research question.

There are some codes that are not going to have anything to do with what it is that you are researching which are going to help you either drop or tie the data into a common theme. The common themes are going to be open to the organized theme that you are working on which then is going to lead to one global theme. The global theme tied to your analysis will usually show an illustration of the research that you did to answer the question that you started studying.

3. Methods for your quantitative data

When you have collected data, there will be some typical forms that you are going to see in your data.

- Scores or rankings
- Units
- Rates of change
- Pricing
- Percentages

The analysis that is done will be used to create a summary of the numerical data for a visualization aid like a chart or graph.

Most of the quantitative data that is obtained will come in a wide variety of forms based on the sources that were used in your research.

- Services offered by a provider or the assessments done at a facility: these are often carried out whenever the participants are under supervision.
- Surveys and questionnaires: these methods are typically going to have questions that are constructed based on a ranking system where the answers are scored. The questions may also be close-ended questions where the respondent is limited to a certain number of answers that they can choose from.
- The service provider or data from a facility: you can pull data from a health care clinic such as records for the children that were vaccinated or from a school of their attendance for that week.

- Biophysical measurements: things such as height and weight.

- Project records: these are going to be some of the best resources for data. These files are going to be things such as a training event that a school holds and how many people actually attend.

BONUS - Business Intelligence

In this bonus chapter you will learn valuable insights and priceless info. This chapter in particular will be especially beneficial to those current or future business owners and potential entrepreneurs alike. Whether you are in the preliminary stages of planning your business or at launch stage, the information contained within this chapter will greatly aid you and perhaps even open your eye to new opportunities you may have not seen before. Let's get to it.

Business intelligences encompasses a wide range of factors such as discerning markets, laws, accounting and management. First off when we discuss business, and I mean any kind of business we must address two fundamental elements. *Mindset* and *Systems*. Now this may not sound like a secret formula to make a fortune, but hear me out. In order to operate any successful business, we need to get our mindset right, and in particular the way we think must take a drastic shift from employee to owner mentality. Meaning we want to "work on our business" and "not work in your business". Understand the differences, working in your business connotes your caught up internally and actually work like any other employee. Working on your business takes more of an ownership role, and although you do not directly engage in the business, however you control it from afar and make crucial decisions.

One's perception about money tells you a lot. I'll elaborate, employees work for money, but business owners make money work for them. We need to get down to the psychology of money, and in reality money is just an illusion, and in essence we give money value as a medium or vehicle in which we engage in commerce. Employees think " how can I work to get more money?", and look for opportunities with benefits and job security. Business owners think " How can I make money work for me?", and exponentially make it grow. There are clear and distinct differences between both perceptions, and obviously one is definitely more favorable than the other.

Moving on to "systems". Earlier I discussed setting your mindset in the right way and making a drastic shift from employee to owner mentality. Now we must discuss systems and how to properly leverage systems found within businesses. Do you recall when I mentioned the phrase " make money work for you", I am referring to having systems in place that generates revenue for you consistently and on a perpetual basis. If you wanted to learn how to play basketball, how would you go about doing this? You would most likely need to learn the body mechanics involved, rules and regulations, interact with your teammates, practice drills, get coaching and learn gameplay strategies. What I just described here was a system, and this system would teach you the ins and outs of the game of basketball from beginning to end.

Now how does this translate into real world business? Well, much in the same way, I'll elaborate.

In order to run a business you need to have mechanisms, techniques/strategies, employees, and colleagues in place. First off, we would need to establish and define what our market is and if there is a demand for it. Secondly, we would need to outsource work to suppliers, assuming this is a retail business. Once we've established a chosen product, market and a reliable supplier we are ready to go to the next phase.

The very backbone for any business is marketing and sales . You would need to learn marketing or hire someone who knows how to market your product or services to a specific target audience. Honing your marketing capacities is essential for the survival of any business, and especially in this digital age where there are so many platforms in which you can leverage marketing to your target demographics.

Next, you need allies meaning build strong rapport with highly intelligent professionals, such as accountants and lawyers. Ask for their advice and insights and you would be surprised at how much progress you can make when you put more minds together. The purpose of having these professionals is to help you navigate through complex regulations, frameworks and legal jargon that you may have no knowledge of. Once this is all done you can start looking to hire reliable employees/managers to work for you. This part is just as crucial as any other component of the business model because a good employee can make or break your business too. This in essence is how you run a retail business, and once you have a system solidified in place you can expect recurring income that is essentially automatic. The initial start up phase will always be the hardest and take the most effort, but once things start to fall in place gradually you will be able to "make money work for you".

Different Types of Investments/ Businesses Models

In this sub chapter I'd like to discuss different types of investments and business models. First, let's talk about investing. When I say investing what is the first thing that comes to mind? Perhaps real estate, stocks, and bonds? Well, yes those are definitely investments depending on the circumstance. Before I go into detail about investing I'd like to discuss a crucial point, and that's knowing the differences between assets and liabilities. The reason why I am doing this is because before you may even start to think about making investments you need to ensure you have a proper understanding of assets and liabilities.

Whether you believe it or not, the vast majority of society does not really understand the distinct differences between an asset and liability. There is a reason why the growing gap between the poor and rich continually increases and this is due to lack of financial literacy. The poor tend to spend their hard earned dollars on depreciating assets or liabilities, while the rich invest their money into asset generating income. For instance, imagine someone wins a small fortune from the lottery. Perhaps 25 grand what do you think a poor person would do versus a rich person? Most likely spend it on a new car, designer clothes, expensive dinners and maybe even jewelry. Now these luxuries are nice and I have nothing against them if its within your means to afford it. However, upon further inspection we can see this person just squandered his money. I'll explain, as soon as you purchase a vehicle and step foot into it, the initial value has already decreased. Did you know when you step foot into a brand new car and use it for the first time, it has already depreciated by 5%-10% of its original value. Than generally speaking it depreciates at the rate of 15%-20% per year subsequently.

Now let's take a look at what a rich person would do with 25k. He or she would most likely look to invest in stocks, perhaps platinum, oil, and even cryptocurrencies like bitcoin. Speaking of which, if you want to learn about bitcoins and how to invest in them I would totally recommend you read the following book written by Raymond Kazuya, "Bitcoin & Cryptocurrencies Guide". Please see link below.

Link: http://amzn.to/2tRQpyj

A rich person would also probably start a business with the 25k. He or she would study markets and trends and from that information draw out a business plan and execute. Remember the rich rent luxuries and spend on assets that generate income, but the poor only spend to own liabilities and do not invest in assets. Can you see the polar opposite mindsets and habits? The rich make every effort to stay rich and are in it for the long haul, but the poor only attempt to look rich and slowly deteriorate. Thus, the importance of having a good financial literacy and understanding of money, assets, and liabilities before you start investing.

It's time to look into different types of online business models. I personally chosen the most practical and easiest entry points which are online business models people can get into. Almost anyone can get into these types of ventures with very little start up costs.

Affiliate Marketing - This business model is one of my favorites as you don't deal with inventory or have to create a product. It's all online, and you take a product that already exists and push it to the consumer, and when you make a sale you get a percentage of commission for that product sold. This is a very scalable business model, but you do have to be a little tech savvy, and understand the fundamentals of marketing, and how to effectively find your target audiences. My advice is if you get into this type of business model aim high and go hard. Meaning you need to push "high ticket products" in order to be extremely successful. There are both sides of the story to this low ticket and high ticket paradigm, and yes you can still making quite a substantial amount of money off the low ticket products, but why choose quantity over quality? See below the difference between high and low ticket products (Quality vs Quantity)

Low ticket product (quantity) - these products are generally below $100 and someone using these tactics is depending on quantity of products sold in order to generate a substantial amount of revenue. The good thing is affordable products equates to more sales, however the downside is the commission you make off it and the number of sales you need to make a decent living. So when you're doing product launches its more work for you in the long run and could potentially drain you. Also up selling will have a very low conversion rate for low end products and this is just the nature of the clientele.

High ticket product (quality) - These products are on the higher end $500+ and although it is quite the price tag for the average person you need to look at the long run. This type of demographic is extremely valuable and a lot easier to up sell too. They are more likely to convert and buy other related products and are simply more receptive to new deals, offers and bargins.

Now let's compare and contrast both high and low ticket products. Now let's say you make 15% per commission off a product, how much do you think you can make off a low end product? So for instance you sell a $9 product, and this equates to a $1.35 commission per sale, these are peanuts. Versus a $500 product sold at 15% commission which equates to a $75 commission per sale. Now this is not a fortune but, its far greater than its counterpart. If you took the low ticket product route at a $1.35 commission you would need 56 sales to catch up to 1 high ticket product sale!

The difference is vast and the better choice is obvious. With high ticket products you are engaging high quality customers, and let's face it generally speaking customers who are only willing to spend money on low end products will not make you rich! Also after taxes with $1.35 you're not really left with much. The point here is QUALITY over QUANTITY.

Drop shipping/Private Labeling - These business models are a bit more advanced and can get complicated. Let's start off by discussing drop shipping, what is drop shipping? You essentially own an online store (website) and you sell any product you want. You find a supplier through sites like Alibaba, Aliexpress, Global sources, Trade key, etc. - Do your own research before attempting to use any of these mentioned sites. You want to decide what type of product you will be selling and once you find a reliable supplier you fulfill an order through them and buy your products in bulk, which then gets shipped to a fulfillment center, which stores your items awaiting to be delivered to your customers.

There are fees associated with delivery and storage, so these must be taken into account for costs when deciding your selling price. The product you buy will most likely range from $1-$10 each. Thus, you want to mark up the price so you make a tidy profit. Dropping shipping operates similarly to any retail store, except you don't deal with inventory. Key considerations to remember; where are you purchasing from? -Who is your supplier? How long will products take to be shipped? - Usually if it's from China your waiting anywhere between 4-8 weeks and sometimes more! This can be an extremely stressful, and expect delays and perhaps even mismatched products sent to your customer. Customers WILL get impatient, so if you know a certain product will take long to arrive, don't take chances. The last thing you want is an angry customer who leaves a 1 star review, which can potentially destroy your business.

Speaking of reviews, you will need to set a budget aside for FREE promo launches and give your products out for free so some customers can potentially give you reviews. -This is also an essential component and crucial to ranking your product and will dictate the longevity of its selling rate and survival of your business.

Lastly advertising, you will need to learn how to leverage marketing tools such as Facebook to target specific audiences for your products. There are various resources on the internet that show you how to use Facebook ads. You essentially want to narrow down your demographics from gender, interests, and geographical location. The more specific the better in this line of business, wide range shot gun approaches are not necessarily the best thing to do! If you're like most people and have a limited budget you would just be burning your hard earned dollars.

So this was the gist of drop shipping and it can be quite a strenuous effort and big investment upfront. But if you master this business model and do get good at it your looking anywhere between *50,000 - 150,000* revenue at a 35% profit margin per month, which equates to roughly **19,000 - 52,000** net profit per month! That's after all your expenses on advertising, product purchase, shipping and storage costs. That's easily a six figure business all done at the click of a few buttons at the comfort of your home. - Note: It takes a lot of work and is not as easy as pushing a few buttons here and there. Stay away from hefty items and electronics as there are a lot of things that can go wrong with these types of products. Heavy items will incur you excess costs due to weight for shipping, and electronics can easily break from oversee travels, thus rendering damaged goods and refunded items, which is a double whammy to your business expenses.

Private Labeling - This business model is an interesting one in particular. You must first define your parameters, market, product and demographics. You will than select a product online, and ensure its a product that is not patented! Aim for products that will cost you between $10-$50 when starting out as you want to keep expenses low and mitigate any other potential pitfalls down the road, such as damaged goods or returned products from unsatisfied customers. Once you've selected a product you are ready for the next step.

Let's use a yoga mat for example as the selected product. Similar to drop shipping you will be utilizing fulfillment storage centers, and you want to aim for products under 5lb, remember the heavier the product the more you will be charged for delivery! Also, my advice is until you hone your talents and master this business model do not do electronic items. Now you have a chosen product it's time to contact your supplier or manufacturer, and you ask them to attach your own company logo to the desired product. (assuming you have a company)

 Now you have a product with a brand that you OWN. Similar to drop shipping you will need to market, get reviews through give aways, do FREE promos and product launches. You will need to assess the competition and compete with people within your budget and league. Look for low competition and search for specific market niches.

High Level Corporate Marketing Consulting - This is one of my favorite models and is an advanced one. You really got to know your stuff, niches, and have ample marketing experience, intimately know your clientele and have brand presence. What does a corporate marketing consultant do? Your job is essentially to drive more sales, revenue and business growth for a company that contracts your marketing expertise and services. This is where your marketing skills would shine and you would use various marketing tools, platforms, SEO strategies, etc.

You must have a professional appearance, demeanor and a website that entails your services, and also having testimonial proofs of people who can vouch for you. Perhaps someone who can be a lead referral too. Considering the digital age we live in there are so many multi-million dollar companies getting left behind in marketing and the current digital trend. A lot of these "old school " and archaic companies do not know how to leverage the power of social media! It was Charles

Darwin who said " It's not the strongest who survive, but it's those who are able to adapt". What happened to companies like Kodak (camera company that used film) ? they couldn't adapt and hop onto the trends fast enough. Digital cameras were the new hype, and this had a significant impact negatively on this film roll based photography company.

As a marketing consultant you are the agent or intermediary who is the sole driving force of generating revenue. You will utilize social media such as Facebook, Instagram, Twitter, and Pinterest. You will discover ways to increase efficiencies, sales, and drive massive traffic. A corporate consultant can make anywhere between *10,000 - 50,000+* per client! This could be over a 4 month, 6 month or even a 12 month period. Your aim as an online marketer is to produce long lasting results helping the company you have been contracted to work for reach the next stage of business and growth. The amount of work you get is dependent on your track record of success and if you can actually produce massive results. Again, this is strongly recommended for people who are extremely advanced in online marketing, tech savvy and who have strong work ethic.

Real Estate - Lastly I wanted to add one last business model, the real estate industry. Some consider it an indestructible industry and one of the most scalable. The reason I decided to mention this industry in the list of "online business models" is because a lot of skills overlap and are easily transferable. I want to keep your mind open for opportunities down the road. What is real estate? Without trying to complicate things and give you a convoluted definition, let's just say real estate is essentially selling "high ticket products".

Depending on what country, city or whatever geographical location you reside within regulations, rules and policies differ place to place. So it's up to you to be informed and do your own research and stay up to date. This is definitely a lucrative industry and perhaps one of the most competitive . But let's dissect some fundamentals of real estate, so you can better understand what it is. Earlier I discussed high ticket products and vouched for quality over quantity. Well guess what? Real estate operates on the same exact principles, and these "houses" is what you consider high ticket products.

Of course this is a highly regulated industry which contains many regulatory frameworks that are set in place that you must abide by and be aware of. Again, due to the nature and scope of this industry differing from country to country I cannot give you exact details as it will differ from one geographical location to another. But, the fundamentals are essentially the same to affiliate marketing. You find a market and a product that already exists, and in this case a house and the housing/condo industry. You push a the product and make a sale, and get a commission off it. Therefore, you get a house sold and earn a commission on it. Now this type of commission is far greater than 99% of affiliate marketing products you will be able to find.

You can consider this a top of the line commission. So how much can you make? Well, I'll give you an example. If you deal with a high value demographic and sell a 1.5 million dollar house at a low end *%2* commission you will receive a $30,000 commission for that one sale! That's more money than some people make in a year! Incredible right?

(0.02 x 1500000 = 30,000)

Business Intelligence Continued..

As you can see shifting your mindset and leveraging systems is how everyone can make a fortune. Is it easy? Well, that depends on your skill level, commitment and work ethic. All I can say is it takes a lot of work and it's a process, and not overnight, and definitely not a get rich quick scheme.

So why the emphasis on online businesses? The scalability is massive and the entry point allows almost anyone with a internet connection to jump in on the bandwagon. The internet is a beautiful thing, literally connecting the world together, and expanding your horizons in regards to business. You can easily outsource work to cut costs, generate sales from outside your native land, and have layers and layers of protection encrypted by cyberspace. Over 3 billion people have access to the internet, with the internet you open up a global economy at the palm of your hands. -Imagine that all this from using a computer or laptop from home.

20-30 years ago you would need some serious funding to start any business venture, perhaps 100k. But if you opt for an online business you have very little start up costs and a low barrier entry point. Very low risk.

Net Worth

I'm sure you heard of the term "net worth" before? But what does it actually mean? Net worth is an evaluation of your current value after expenses. Essentially, gauging your total assets and your worth. Knowing your net worth and real value is actually a crucial component to business intelligence, and we'll soon see why.

You see there's a lot of people who claim to make millions or perhaps even six figures, but what is there actual net worth? It's very misleading to evaluate someone's value based on their generated revenue, and believe it or not a lot of people use this tactic to sell business plans, seminars and courses! It's not very honest or ethical to do so, and I'm going to show you how to find out one's true net worth and spot the deception.

For instance let's say John owns a drop shipping business and generates $10,000 in revenue a month. However, delivery fees, cost of production, storage fees, and marketing campings add up to $9,500 in total expenses. John's net worth after expenses would be valued at only *$500*. How did we arrive at this conclusion? Please see my break down $10,000 revenue minus 9,500 expenses equates to a total of $500 net worth. So it would be very misleading of John to claim he makes 10k profit a month, which is not at all true!

Net worth reveals the true value of a person's business, and in this case John's drop shipping business is only worth $500, despite the substantial amount of revenue he generated. Therefore, remember this formula *Assets - Liabilities = net worth.* (A-L = Net)

The take home message here is not only to learn how to accurately determine one's net worth, but continually develop and accumulate assets that generate revenue, which in turn would increase your overall net worth.

Conclusion

Thank you for making it through to the end of *Data Analytics Guide: For Beginners Introduction*, let's hope it was informative and able to provide you with all of the tools you need to achieve your goals whatever it may be.

The next step is to take what you have learned here and begin to use it so that you can not only have better analysis when it comes to your data, but also so that you can make yourself valuable to your company that you are working for. Or, so that you can find a new job if that is what you are looking to do in order to advance in your goals.

Keep in mind that data analysis is not going to be easy and it is going to take a lot of time as well as patience for you to get the hang of it, but you are going to be able to do it. The important thing to remember is that there are going to be risks, but you should not allow those risks to stop you from doing your job. You are not only going to be making your job better, but you are going to be able to make other people's lives better.

Data analysis is in the world around us every day and we should not take it for granted due to the fact that what we see in the store is going to be there because of data that was gathered and analyzed to see if that product did good in the store or not. Not only that, but it also helps to improve products so that they are not in their first stages. Take a look at iPhone for example. There has been an iPhone released at least every other year with new features that the customer said they wanted on their phones. The same thing goes for when the phone updates. It is updating to improve applications and functions on the phone so that it runs better for their consumer. The same goes for the products that you find in the store. That is another reason why you can go to two different stores that are in the same franchise and find assorted products, it is not always demographics. It is based on the data that the company gets in what is bought in that community.

Hopefully thanks to this book, you are going to have a better understanding of data analytics and how it works in the world around you. If you picked up this book, it was obviously because you wanted to know more about data analysis so that you can change jobs or because you want to become better at the job that you already have. No matter what your reason is, good luck and thank you for picking up this book!

Finally, if you found this book useful in any way, a review on Amazon or on the site in which you purchased it is always appreciated!

Thank you and good luck!

www.ingramcontent.com/pod-product-compliance
Lightning Source LLC
Chambersburg PA
CBHW071924080326
R17960400001B/R179604PG40689CBX00018B/15